MW01485738

SAWDUST IN YOUR POCKETS

Sawdust in Your Pockets

A HISTORY OF THE NORTH CAROLINA FURNITURE INDUSTRY

Eric Medlin

UNIVERSITY OF GEORGIA PRESS ▲▼ ATHENS

© 2023 by the University of Georgia Press
Athens, Georgia 30602
www.ugapress.org
All rights reserved
Designed by Melissa Buchanan
Set in Chapparal Pro

Most University of Georgia Press titles are
available from popular e-book vendors.

Printed digitally

Library of Congress Cataloging-in-Publication Data
Names: Medlin, Eric, author.
Title: Sawdust in your pockets : a history of the North Carolina
furniture industry / Eric Medlin.
Description: Athens : University of Georgia Press, [2023] | Includes
bibliographical references and index.
Identifiers: LCCN 2023020935 (print) | LCCN 2023020936 (ebook) |
ISBN 9780820365510 (hardback) | ISBN 9780820365503 (paperback) |
ISBN 9780820365527 (epub) | ISBN 9780820365534 (pdf)
Subjects: LCSH: Furniture industry—North Carolina—History.
Classification: LCC HD9773.U53 N864 2023 (print) |
LCC HD9773.U53 (ebook) | DDC 338.4/7684109756—dc23/eng/20230615
LC record available at https://lccn.loc.gov/2023020935
LC ebook record available at https://lccn.loc.gov/2023020936

CONTENTS

ACKNOWLEDGMENTS

Writing this book has been a four-year undertaking and has consumed countless hours of typing, travel, and research. I could not have done it on my own, however. There are many people to thank at all stages of the process. First, I absolutely must thank Michael R. Hill, Michael Coffey, and the staff at the North Carolina Division of Historical Publications for helping give me the idea of this book in the first place. Mr. Hill was the one who told me that there had not yet been a book on the furniture industry and prompted me to write one. I am forever grateful for his insight and help throughout the writing process.

On the research side, I am indebted to the hardworking staff and researchers at the various archives I visited in the past few years. Karla Jones at the Bienenstock Furniture Library in High Point guided me throughout every stage of the process and also served as an invaluable source in sharing what she learned from her time in the industry. Karla at Bienenstock also helped me compile records and reach out to several leaders in the industry. Other helpful partners at research institutions have been Ross Cooper at Appalachian State University; Taylor De Klerk and Matthew Turi at the North Carolina Collection, Wilson Library, University of North Carolina at Chapel Hill; Erin Fulp and Vann Evans at the North Carolina State Archives; Beth Hayden at the State Library of North Carolina; and Lucy Vanderkamp and Kelsey Zavelo at the David M. Rubenstein Rare Book and Manuscript Library.

Several members of the furniture industry donated their time to help my research. Alex Shuford, president and CEO of Century Furniture, graciously allowed me to tour the company's factory and took the time to talk with me about the business. I am also indebted to Tom Burke of Tomlinson Erwin-Lambeth and David Williams of Wits End Design Studio for bringing me into their segments of the furniture industry and allowing me to view and ask questions about their work. Kay Lambeth of Tomlinson Erwin-Lambeth, Abu Bakr Khan of Abu Rugs and Home, and

Charles Sutton of Sutton Fine Furniture all provided helpful insights into the furniture business. As for images, I am grateful to the Museum of Early Southern Decorative Arts, the North Carolina Museum of History, the Forest History Society, the Wake Forest School of Law, and Somerset Place for their generous help in compiling and securing permissions for the images included in this book.

I am also grateful to Nate Holly, Lisa Bayer, my reviewers, and the staff at the University of Georgia Press for their help in reading and preparing the manuscript. Susan Rodriguez served as a first reader, copyedited the book, and created the index. I am forever in debt to her hard work and careful, determined eye. Finally, I would like to thank my mother, Julia Medlin, whose belief in me helped make this project possible.

SAWDUST IN YOUR POCKETS

When learning about the twentieth-century North Carolina economy, students from elementary school to graduate school encounter three signature industries: textiles, tobacco, and furniture. They learn that North Carolina embraced manufacturing earlier than most southern states and that it became an industrial center, comparable even to the Rust Belt and New England states. While the textile and tobacco industries have certainly received their due from historians and the general public over the past century, the furniture industry has been strangely ignored.

North Carolina's textile legacy is well known and well established. Northern mills moved south in the late nineteenth and early twentieth centuries, bringing jobs to North Carolina that defined the state's place in the New South. Textile magnates like William Edwin Holt, Moses H. Cone, and James Cannon built massive factories and dominated society in much of North Carolina. The story of these factories and their impact on the state has been told time and again. From the early sociological studies of Harriet L. Herring and Howard Odum to the dramatic labor confrontations at Loray Mill and the ordinary textile mill lives portrayed in *Like A Family* (1987) by Jacquelyn Dowd Hall and her colleagues, the textile industry in North Carolina is arguably the best-studied aspect of the state's history. The state's textile heritage has also influenced popular culture with mill village country music and movies like *Norma Rae* telling the story of North Carolina's mills to the entire world.

Tobacco had a similar impact. Titans in tobacco such as R. J. Reynolds and James B. Duke became nearly as famous as their contemporaries in the North. The institutes of higher learning set up by these men, Wake Forest University and Duke University, are globally famous. The tobacco products themselves can be found all over the world. As Milton Ready notes in his history of North Carolina, cigarettes produced by these companies were arguably more popular in the North than the South at first: "easy to carry, 'quick and potent,' slim, and aesthetically an extension of the index finger, cigarettes suited the new urban market of the Northeast. Immigrants from Europe soon took up the habit."[1] The tobacco industry itself has been the subject of much historical research, most notably Robert Korstad's *Civil Rights Unionism: Tobacco Workers and the Struggle for Democracy in the Mid-Twentieth-Century South* (2003). In the realm of culture, tobacco inspired the famous 1964 song "Tobacco Road" and played a role in the 1988 hit movie *Bull Durham*.

Surprisingly, furniture has been mostly ignored by the same forces that have lavished such attention on tobacco and textiles. The state is known as a center of furniture, and many are familiar with the High Point Market. But no significant study has been undertaken, especially not one to rival *Like a Family* or *Civil Rights Unionism*.[2] The scholarly articles and books on the industry are negligible. There are, in fact, more histories of the North Carolina gold industry, a thirty-year venture that created only a fraction of the wealth that furniture did. Furniture's titans of industry, with the possible exception of James Broyhill, are not famous and are nowhere near household names. Parents know of High Point University because of its pristine campus and its president, not its connections to the furniture industry. There is no *Bull Durham* for High Point and no well-known songs about life in Thomasville or Hickory.

This omission is glaring. At its height, the North Carolina furniture industry employed nearly one million people at hundreds of different sites in the Piedmont and mountains. Companies such as Broyhill, Thomasville, and Drexel were among the largest in North Carolina and produced furniture that was exported all around the world. The state led production in nearly every kind of furniture and became well known for durable, inexpensive pieces as well as the finest produced in the country. North Carolina shaped design trends, pioneered the use of new materials, and slowly took over from Michigan and Illinois as the nation's furniture leader. The state remains the leading furniture manufacturer in the nation, even after three decades of plant closures and the loss of most case goods factories.

My book seeks to give furniture its long overdue credit. It is the first published book-length survey of the North Carolina furniture industry; unlike earlier work, it does not take up only a single company or time period but has a sweeping scope, beginning with the seventeenth century and moving through to the present day. I argue that the furniture industry certainly deserves its reputation in textbooks as a pillar of the North Carolina economy. I tell the story of furniture through the companies and people in the business, both those who sat at the executives' table and those who worked on the shop floor. I look at the economic impact on the state and on the furniture belt, a term for the furniture-producing region of the state that included counties from Alamance in the east to Burke in the west.[3] I also study how the industry expanded across the globe and how its labor force changed over time, starting out as a white male enterprise but eventually admitting women and African Americans.

Along the way, I inevitably make a number of comparisons to the state's contemporaneous textile industry. The history of the textile industry sets the standard for industrial histories in North Carolina. It had everything: political intrigue, robber barons, communists, crusading sociologists, martyrs, plagues, and a tragic collapse. Students of North Carolina know the names of its heroes and villains by heart: Ella Mae Wiggins the labor organizer, Walter Hines Page the public health crusader, James Cannon the latter-day lord of his manor in Kannapolis.[4] Books on the textile industry have won several major awards in the fields of sociology, history, and cultural studies; in 2004, *Civil Rights Unionism* won the Charles S. Sydnor Award for best book of southern history, while in 1988 *Like a Family* won the Albert J. Beveridge Award for best American history book as well as the Merle Curti History Award in American social history and the Philip Taft Labor History Award.

While there are no canonical works about the furniture industry and it lacks prestige among historians, it resembles the textile business. Many towns in North Carolina, such as Hickory and High Point, had both robust furniture factories and a sizable textile industry.[5] Both had factory towns and paid their workers poorly throughout much of the twentieth century. Textiles, of course, are frequently used in upholstered furniture, and there have been important symbiotic relationships between textile and furniture companies throughout the state's history.

However, one of my implicit arguments in this book is that the furniture industry, for one reason or another, has always been less dramatic and more staid than the textile industry. As a smaller, slightly less prosperous, and less domineering industry, it has been subject to many of the same forces as textiles, but their effect has been less intense. While textile companies gave the state numerous governors, furniture company executives only captured one Senate seat and one lieutenant governorship. Textile and furniture companies both had strikes, but only textile strikes led to a war that captured the public's imagination. Tracing out these comparisons and exploring the reasons for the different trajectories of these two industries helps ground this book in the historiography of North Carolina industry and creates a framework for understanding a previously understudied field.

The two key histories of the textile industry in North Carolina, *Like a Family* and Brent Glass's *The Textile Industry in North Carolina: A History* (1992), are the primary models for my work. *Like a Family* tells the story of an industry and the interpersonal connections of workers with each other and their bosses. It is famous for its innovative methodology and the years of oral history work that went into its completion.[6] Glass's work is more of a brief history that attempts to, in the author's words, provide "a selective and occasionally idiosyncratic overview designed to provide the thematic framework for a more comprehensive study."[7] My book hews closer to the Glass model in aiming to use primary sources, analytical concepts, and case studies to tell the story of the industry and its impact on the history of a state. I do, however, also use a wide variety of oral histories from both leaders and workers in the industry.

While the twentieth century is the main focus, this book does take a close look at the industry's colonial and nineteenth-century antecedents. North Carolina has been in some ways a center of furniture making ever since the arrival of English immigrants in the seventeenth century. My book traces how early craftsmen grew more sophisticated and how earlier, lesser-known figures contributed to the work of famed artisans such as Thomas Day. These artisans used new technology as well as slave labor to produce famous pieces that adorned the homes of North Carolina's wealthiest citizens and leaders, and their status in the community influenced North Carolina's laws, politics, and reputation.

Following the Civil War, the prefactory age gave way to the High Point furniture boom, which turned the formerly sleepy Piedmont town into an industrial powerhouse in a little over a decade. Nearly half of this book covers the golden age of the furniture industry, roughly from the 1920s to the early 1990s. In this period, furniture companies gained international influence. Factories grew to sizes that dwarfed their nineteenth-century antecedents. Highways and new manufacturing processes helped the industry expand to new towns and ship to faraway locales. Large conglomerates attempted to take over the furniture industry with mixed results. As one local furniture executive said to a *Fortune* magazine reporter when asked about large-company interlopers, "You can't understand furniture until you have your pockets filled with sawdust and your mouth full of tobacco juice."[8]

The industry diversified during the period as well, resisting and then grudgingly accepting African Americans and women into its plants and management ranks. Industry made gains along with the Southern Furniture Market, which began in 1909 and became a biannual pilgrimage to the furniture belt for buyers, designers, and celebrities alike. Furniture played a key role in the state's culture during this time. Through the construction of monuments and the establishment of baseball teams, furniture made its mark on an ever-prosperous region of North Carolina, an influence that spread north and west past the state's boundaries.

Finally, I show how the development of industry led to diversification and service-sector growth that positioned the industry for success after the traumas of the 1990s. Plant closures forced the industry to find a niche that has allowed it to remain relevant up to the present day. I argue that, ironically, even though it was the smallest of North Carolina's three largest industries, furniture fared better in the twenty-first century than textiles or tobacco.

I have written this book in the hope that it will propel future scholarship in this field, as it is ripe for study. The industry speaks to a number of issues—material culture, the history of natural resources, unions, workers' rights, and race relations—that have been immensely popular with historians over the past four decades. Dozens of notable companies, unique towns, and key incidents provide case studies that could occupy historians and graduate students for years. I intend for this book to be a starting point and a call to action for these studies.

But in filling a glaring gap in the historical record of North Carolina this book has a purpose outside of the academy as well, which is to tell the story of North Carolina's furniture workers and executives. The ten largest counties of the furniture belt are home to approximately two million people as of 2020. A significant percentage of these people either worked in furniture or have parents, grandparents, uncles, and aunts associated with furniture in some form or fashion. These North Carolinians need the story of furniture told to give context to their histories and their place in society. This volume takes the first step in documenting this past.

CHAPTER ONE ▲▼

Artisans Large and Small

THE BEGINNINGS OF THE NORTH CAROLINA
FURNITURE INDUSTRY UP TO 1865

The roots of the North Carolina furniture industry can be traced back to
English colonization in the mid-seventeenth century. After the Roanoke
colony failed, more permanent settlers began to trickle into the Albe-
marle region from Virginia starting in the 1650s. The colonial population, while small at first, exploded after the Tuscarora War (1711–13). By
the 1760s, North Carolina was one of the most populous North American
colonies. Its residents founded small towns like Edenton, Bath, and New
Bern and mainly cultivated corn and tobacco.

The men and women of North Carolina needed furniture, and importing it was complicated. The coastline included the Outer Banks, a treach-
erous stretch of barrier islands that made oceangoing travel difficult.
There were no wide, deep ports like those in Charleston and the Ches-
apeake Bay. Settlers in North Carolina had to rely on smaller ports such
as Wilmington, Brunswick, and Beaufort that were on the other side of
shifting inlets and sandbars that came and went with every hurricane.
Consequently, acquiring goods such as clothing, furniture, and printed
material from England was a challenge. North Carolina's isolation led to
limited development during the colonial period and smaller quantities of
imported furniture compared with other colonies.

But North Carolina was well situated to develop a domestic furniture
industry of its own. It had several key components required to build, sell,
and transport furniture. The first was abundant forests. The most common type of tree was the pine, of both the loblolly and longleaf varieties,
still the most common today. Pine trees remain abundant in all sections
of the state and were often used to produce sawed lumber as well as furniture. They are easy to saw and form into furniture, although they do
not have the fine grains required for more expensive furniture.

The colony also had a wide variety of other trees suitable for furniture, including hickory, oak, beech, and mulberry as well as maple and walnut, which produced finer woods.[1] Before the widespread production of furniture and lumber, eastern trees were harvested for naval stores. Their tall trunks could be used as masts, and they could be cultivated for tar, pitch, and turpentine. In the eighteenth century, North Carolina became one of the world's leading producers of naval stores, earning the nickname of "tar heels" for its people.

Along with forests, North Carolina had the internal waterways necessary for early furniture production. Water provided power in the form of mill dams and aided in transportation with the use of bateaux. The Haw, Deep, and Dan Rivers provided power to mills of all kinds, including the sawmills used to cut lumber for furniture. Even though North Carolina's international connections were limited, its interior rivers were abundant and facilitated transportation between towns.

The colony also had the labor necessary to launch a furniture industry. The eventual home of the North Carolina furniture industry, the western Piedmont, was settled during the eighteenth century and steadily grew in population. The seven counties in 1790 that most closely corresponded to the later furniture-producing region had a combined population of 61,529, or about 15 percent of the total population of 393,751. By 1860, the seven closest corresponding counties had 94,216 people, which represented a 50 percent increase, even though it was only about 10 percent of the total population. These counties also had relatively low slave populations (averaging 18.5 percent in 1869, lower than the percentage for sixty-four out of eighty-six counties) because of their inhabitants' Quaker background and the poor soil quality, which led to low agricultural returns and thus less of a need for slaves.[2]

Because the western Piedmont yielded lower returns from agriculture, there was a lower opportunity cost to putting aside capital, acquiring machinery, and building a factory, which eventually led to the furniture industry renaissance in the late nineteenth and early twentieth centuries. But during the colonial period, such preeminence was inconceivable. At that time, the highest-quality furniture in North Carolina came from overseas. Wealthy North Carolinians like Edward Moseley and Arthur Dobbs copied their Virginia and South Carolina brethren by importing tables, beds, and dressers in the latest French and English fashions. In a 1726 report on the colonies, Martin Bladen, namesake of North Carolina's Bladen County, notes that "the Luxury of the Colonies which increase daily consumes great Quantities of English Manufactur'd Silks, Haberdashery, Household Furniture and Trinkets of all sorts, also a very considerable Value in E: India Goods."[3] It is clear that furniture followed the same lines of cultural transmission as books, clothing, and political ideas from the Old World to the New.

The inventory lists at Tryon Palace show the kinds of furniture that wealthy North Carolinians had access to in the late colonial period. Tryon Palace was the most famous house in North Carolina at the time, a massive brick structure built for Governor William Tryon in the capital of New Bern. To appoint the house, Tryon ordered tables, chairs, beds, and all sorts of furnishings and decorative pieces from England. When the palace was rebuilt in the 1950s, historians reconstructed the original furniture list from two inventories taken of the palace and Tryon's personal belongings in the 1770s. Two neoclassical tables, a George III mahogany card table, and a number of square elbow chairs as well as pieces from France and China counted among the furniture Tryon imported.[4]

The vast majority of North Carolinians did not have access to the finest furniture from England or France. They did not live in one of the colony's few towns and mainly practiced subsistence agriculture. These men and women produced much of their own furniture as well as their own tools and clothing. If they had the means, they could also buy pieces from colonial artisans, some of whom were located in North Carolina.

Colonial artisans worked in a wide variety of styles. They produced dining and bedroom furniture as well as case goods, a term for bulky unupholstered furniture that includes dressers, bureaus, and desks. They mostly used local woods such as pine or beech, although imported woods were used in pieces dating from the early eighteenth century. Most of this furniture was simple and had basic ornamentation such as leaf designs carved into the wood.

These artisans worked under a wide variety of names and titles. The term "cabinetmaker" is the most familiar to modern audiences and is the trade most associated with the well-known furniture manufacturers of the colonial and antebellum periods. But cabinetmakers were far from the only tradesmen during that time to produce furniture. The term "joiner," referring to the skill of joining wood together, was often used to describe people who made furniture out of wood. Carpenters also produced furniture, although their furniture was typically of lower quality.[5] The main focus of carpenters was work on buildings, hence the term "house carpenter" seen in many colonial records.[6] While "cabinetmaker" usually refers to furniture makers who created particularly high-quality pieces and focused their training on the production of those pieces, cabinetmakers did not typically receive enough commissions to only produce furniture and stay in business. Therefore, they engaged in all sorts of wood-related trades, working as carpenters, coffin makers, and wheelwrights. According to historian John G. Bivins Jr., even some of the best-known cabinetmakers of the colonial period did not practice the craft full-time.[7]

Cabinetmaking and assorted trades such as carpentry and joinery relied on a form of training that dated back to the medieval guild system, a seven-year period of apprenticeship from fourteen to the age of majority. As early as 1693, Jabell Alford, a youth, was ordered to "be bound and enter into bond to learne him the trade of a Carpenter or Joyner" by the Perquimans Precinct Court after Alford petitioned for a guardian (presumably because his parents had died).[8] A master cabinetmaker had near total control over his apprentice and received free labor, and so runaways were a common problem with the system. In 1713 the North Carolina Governor's Council ordered that a runaway apprentice, Stephen Scott, who had been bound to "learne ye trade and mistery of a Carpenter & house Joiner," return to his master cabinetmaker, Thomas Robertson. This decision was not entirely in favor of the master, however, for the council also declared that for the remainder of Scott's apprenticeship Robertson must "not Imoderately correct or abuse ye sd Scott dureing ye Said Services."[9] Once the apprentice reached the end of his indenture, he would be given a suit of apparel and perhaps tools or money and then go on to work for himself in the trade.[10]

Along with making common pieces, artisans like cabinetmakers and joiners also gradually began to copy some aspects of European craftsmanship. They did so with the help of a variety of guidebooks that showed the work of mainly English cabinetmakers. The most famous English cabinetmaker in the New World was Thomas Chippendale, whose *The Gentleman and Cabinet Maker's Director* became the first and arguably most influential trade catalog of a furniture manufacturer. Thomas Sheraton and George Hepplewhite were two other famous names whose guidebooks reached American artisans in the late eighteenth century. Hepplewhite's curved arms and shield-shaped chair backs became influential as did Sheraton's light forms and classical details.[11]

By the mid-eighteenth century, North Carolina artisans were producing works inspired by English masters and styles. They were using imported woods and attaching high-quality veneers onto otherwise simple woods. Their finishes, carving details, and use of glass and paint improved year by year, especially in the colony's towns. In his unpublished history of eastern North Carolina furniture, Alexander Crane describes a number of ornate pieces that an earlier writer, Paul Burroughs, had attributed to local craftsmen. These include a Queen Anne dish-top tea table (circa 1730–50), a Chippendale- and Hepplewhite-inspired card table (circa 1780), and a Chippendale Pembroke table (circa 1770–90), a type of fashionable table with drop leaf sides.[12] Crane remarks that another Chippendale-style side table (1760–70) looked almost exactly like a plate from a Chippendale catalog.[13]

There were also numerous vernacular cabinetmaking traditions in North Carolina, including those of the Quakers as well as the Scots-Irish, who settled in the western Piedmont. There were also the Moravians. These German religious refugees brought centuries of furniture-making traditions with them when they emigrated to present-day Forsyth County in the 1750s, establishing towns such as Salem, Bethabara, and Bethania. Towns located on roads and trading paths facilitated commerce like cabinetmaking more easily than the isolated plantations of the east.

Like eastern and Scots-Irish cabinetmakers, Moravian cabinetmakers had apprenticeship systems.[14] As the Moravian records attest, Thomas Wohlfahrt, for example, took on many young Moravian men (known as brothers) as apprentices; for example, in March 1825 it was recorded that "the Single Brother Jacob Sievers will work under Thomas Wohlfahrt in his cabinet-maker's shop."[15] The apprenticeship system along with the stable nature of Moravian society led to a substantial number of furniture makers in the settlement. When Wohlfahrt applied in 1815 to open up a cabinetmaking shop, he was granted the request on the condition that he work alone, with the Salem Board remarking that "it remains to be seen how three cabinet shops will succeed here."[16] Owing to this oversupply, Moravian cabinetmakers like other cabinetmakers in the colony were forced to do work in other fields. A 1786 letter describing trades in Salem warned that "a glazier and painter would not have enough to do[,] as the cabinet-makers do that work here."[17]

Whether Moravian, Scots-Irish, or Quaker, cabinetmakers traveled extensively throughout the colonies, bringing the mark of their training with them. Several early pieces crafted by North Carolina artisans show the influence of New England manufacturers, who had established their craft in the seventeenth century and were more sophisticated than their southern counterparts. One example of this influence can be seen in the work of Thomas White (d. 1788). A Quaker, White arrived in Perquimans County in 1756 and crafted furniture there for the next ten years. He then moved to Northampton County and married into a wealthy family, becoming one of the largest proprietors in the Rich Square area.[18] There is evidence that White witnessed two marriages in Newport, Rhode Island, and perhaps apprenticed in that town. A side chair attributed to him, currently held by the Museum of Early Southern Decorative Arts (MESDA), has a similar chair back (splat) as that of chairs produced at around the same time in Newport.

The MESDA collection includes dozens of other pieces built in North Carolina prior to 1800 by Moravian and Quaker cabinetmakers as well as those from northeastern North Carolina. It houses one of the earliest southern desk and bookcase combinations. Crafted in Bertie County by local joiner Lawrence Sarson between 1715 and 1730, the elegant desk was owned by numerous people including Cullen Pollock, the son of colonial governor Thomas Pollock. William Seay (Bertie County), David Ruth (Granville County), and Richard Hall (Halifax County) are among other cabinetmakers whose work is represented in the collection. Hall's work is classified as part of the Roanoke River Basin School, which features light wood decorations such as stop fluting and rounded moldings.

Following American independence, North Carolina society changed while its political system remained undeveloped. The state earned the derisive nickname "Rip Van Winkle" for its inattention to infrastructure development and its generally poor, rural character. But social forces were effecting changes that eventually solidified the nebulous furniture industry in the new state. Tobacco and, later, cotton cultivation led to the growth of a planter class, headquartered in counties such as Warren, Martin, and Halifax in the north and New Hanover, Brunswick, and Cumberland in the south. These planters spent their newfound wealth building substantial homes like Somerset Place in Creswell and Hayes Plantation in Edenton. Most significant plantations were in the east, but western farmers also became more prosperous and built stately homes like the famous Blandwood in Guilford County.

Towns increased in size and number throughout the state, with Piedmont towns such as Salisbury, Charlotte, and the new capital of Raleigh expanding alongside New Bern, Tarboro, and Elizabeth City in the east. These towns were connected by rivers and an ever-growing array of roads, joined on occasion by canals and plank roads. Large plantation homes created a demand for high-quality furniture, while towns provided the labor supply, materials, and connections to allow cabinetmaking shops to evolve.

One of the state's largest antebellum woodworking concerns and one of the major precursors to the furniture industry was the wagonmaking industry. Wagonmaking became a force in the 1830s with the Nissen family, whose Moravian patriarch Tycho Nissen arrived in Salem in 1771 and learned the trade from an artisan in the nearby town of Bethania.[19] Tycho's grandson, John Phillip Nissen, opened the Nissen Wagon Works in Salem in 1834 and began a profitable business that lasted for nearly a century. His work was showcased in the 1853 North Carolina State Fair. By 1860, forty-eight wagonmakers who earned at least $500 per year operated throughout the state, producing $82,650 worth of goods. Forsyth County was one of the homes of the state's antebellum wagonmaking industry; it had four sizable wagonmakers whose capital totaled $12,700.[20]

Wagonmaking was a bridge between the cabinetmaking tradition and the furniture industry in North Carolina. By the 1850s, a much higher volume of wagons than cabinets was being produced, as it often took cabinetmakers months to complete a single piece. Wagons were also of lower quality than the highly prized pieces of master cabinetmakers. Wagons were practical and essential for transportation in a growing state. They had an economic purpose as well as an aesthetic one. In this way, they foreshadowed the simple beds, tables, and chairs that were soon to be constructed by the thousands in factories in High Point, Thomasville, and Marion. Wagonmakers also helped the tobacco industry (by hauling tobacco) in much the same way that the furniture industry aided textile companies by providing cheap furniture to workers.

Many of North Carolina's antebellum cabinetmakers were centered in the state's fledgling towns, as they were in the colonial period, and they produced pieces for local plantation owners and middle-class residents. Lewis Bond, an eastern North Carolina cabinetmaker who likely began working in the 1810s, moved from Greenville to Tarboro in 1818. An 1827 newspaper advertisement in nearby Halifax listed Bond's numerous services. He could produce furniture in "New-York or English style" and could make it "plain, or ornamented with carving." The list of pieces Bond could create was considerable. Customers could commission "sideboards, secretaries, book-cases, China-presses, plain Bureaus[,] . . . Tables, Wardrobes, Cabinets, candle Stands, wash Stands." They could also buy one of the dozens of "rush-bottom & stool chairs" or looking-glass plates that Bond had in stock.[21]

Some prominent North Carolinians, such as John Motley Morehead and Josiah Collins II, still imported all of their furniture and continued to do so throughout the nineteenth century.[22] But increasingly, the state's leaders patronized local artisans, especially those of the Roanoke River Basin School, a group of approximately thirty cabinetmakers, the most notable being an anonymous cabinetmaker with the initials "WH" who produced dozens of elegant pieces in the early nineteenth century. Clients of Roanoke River Basin cabinetmakers included Governor David Stone and governor and revolutionary leader Samuel Johnston, who bought a locally made library bookcase for his Edenton plantation.[23] Governor Gabriel Holmes also employed the services of a North Carolina cabinetmaker named C. J. Tooker.[24]

The height of the antebellum North Carolina cabinetmaking industry was captured in the census of 1850. There were 377 cabinetmakers in the state. Thirty-eight cabinetmakers sold enough to appear on the schedules of that year's industrial census, suggesting that most cabinetmakers ran a small shop with few or no hired employees.[25] Several curious features stand out in the census returns of that year. Cabinetmaking shops proliferated in what would become the furniture belt. Out of the 377 cabinetmakers counted, sixty lived in the seven counties that later made up the nucleus of the furniture industry (Burke, Caldwell, Catawba, Iredell, Davidson, Guilford, Randolph). The county with the most cabinetmakers was Rowan, which was a center of Quaker and Moravian cabinetmaking but did not end up developing a major furniture sector in the twentieth century. A large number of cabinetmakers were located outside of the furniture belt. Many counties with more than six cabinetmakers outside of the western Piedmont had a major town, like Craven (twelve, home of New Bern) and Pasquotank (six, home of Elizabeth City).[26]

Like nearly every other North Carolina industry at this time, the furniture industry made ample use of slave labor. Slaves often worked as carpenters, producing and repairing furniture on plantations. Such carpenters were one of many groups of laborers who met the needs of the plantation, along with coopers, blacksmiths, and tailors. A history of enslaved artisans in Virginia notes that the trade of "the slave carpenter comprehended a great many operations. Often such an artisan performed the duties of wheelwright, sawyer, cabinet maker, clapboard maker, cooper, and, in fact, the making of practically anything made of wood."[27] The slave carpenter on a plantation made furniture for both the plantation home and the slave cabins.[28] Some slaves were hired out to other plantations and owners in towns who paid wages to the owner and sometimes the slave. One famous example in Georgia, that of the slave carpenter Woodson, may be representative of urban slave carpenters in North Carolina. Woodson, a slave who originally lived in Savannah, was hired out to work on a plantation house in Georgia and earned income for himself by making furniture.[29]

Free African Americans practiced carpentry and cabinetmaking as well. At numerous times in the pre-Civil War period, the North Carolina legislature passed laws requiring free African American children to become apprentices and learn a trade. While cabinetmaking was a rarer occupation, carpenters at this time often made furniture, and carpentry proved to be a popular choice.[30] Historian John Hope Franklin counted four free African American carpenters and one cabinetmaker in the state with more than $2,500 in property as of 1860.[31] While details on his life and work are sparse, James Sampson of Wilmington possibly made furniture at some points and amassed wealth valued at $36,000, making him the wealthiest free African American in the state in 1860.[32] When they made furniture, many of these carpenters, like their white counterparts, produced pieces for local plantation owners and middle-class citizens.

By far the most influential antebellum artisan in the state was a free African American, Thomas Day (1801–61). Day was born in Dinwiddie County, Virginia, and learned the trade of cabinetmaking from his father. He established a shop in Hillsborough in 1821 but soon moved to Milton, where he remained until he died.[33] Day produced furniture, coffins, and interior architectural elements from his shop in town, which moved to the impressive Union Tavern in 1848. He advertised himself as a repairer and refinisher of furniture as well as a reliable producer of "new furniture that would please customers of various economic means."[34] By 1850, Day was the largest cabinetmaker in the state.[35]

Dozens of Day's pieces survive today in museums and in stately homes across North Carolina. These works show both his attachment to standard forms and his idiosyncratic personal style. A typical example is the sideboard that Day built for Caswell County planter Caleb Richmond between 1840 and 1855. This piece, made of mahogany and mahogany veneer, has numerous details and a symmetry that point to the Greek revival style of cabinetmaking. But the truly outstanding aspect of the piece is the large S-scroll on each side of the main mirror. The dramatic, swooping scroll shows Day's love of fluidity and elegant curls, an attachment that also appears in the many stair posts that he designed for local homebuilders.[36] It was this mix of personal style with conventional attention to detail that made Day such a sought-after cabinetmaker.[37]

Day was also one of the first cabinetmakers to make use of new technology in the field of furniture manufacturing, such as a mechanized circular saw that could cut a plank in less than a minute, much faster than an artisan with a handsaw.[38] His shop contained a six-horsepower engine that powered the circular saw as well as a jigsaw, lathe, and planer.[39] Mechanization made it possible for Day to produce at greater volume, especially architectural woodwork, and his powered jigsaw enabled many intricately carved designs. But this use of technology led to a slight decline of quality in his traditional furniture pieces akin to that in the wagonmaking industry. In their book about Day, Patricia Marshall and Jo Leimenstoll note that some of the furniture Day built soon after receiving the steam engine "displays evidence of haste in construction," such as unfinished drawer bottoms.[40]

Day made a number of political connections and wealthy, powerful friends, which was unique both for a free African American and for a cabinetmaker. The 1829 debate over whether Day should be allowed to bring his new wife, a Virginian, into the state showed the unusual power he wielded. The move would have violated a new North Carolina law banning free African Americans from entering the state. His supporters in Milton feared he might move to Virginia to be with his wife and take his business with him. So they started a campaign to win him an exception to the law, writing a petition to the general assembly testifying to his reputation as a "remarkably sober, steady and industrious man." They were bolstered by then state attorney general Romulus Saunders, who submitted a statement along with the petition noting that he had "known Thomas Day (on whose behalf the within petition is addressed) for several years past" and that he considered "him a free man of color of very fair character, an excellent mechanic, industrious, honest and sober in his habits," adding that "in the event of any disturbance amongst the blacks," he would "rely with confidence upon a disclosure from him, as he is the owner of slaves as well as of real estate."[41] The campaign succeeded. In 1830, the general assembly passed a law specifically allowing his wife to enter the state.[42] It was the only exception to the law that the state passed.

Day's craftsmanship and wealth play a role in his legacy. This legacy is also defined by the nature of his labor force. Day hired whites and free African Americans, making his workforce uniquely diverse. Two Moravians arrived in Day's shop in 1838, a cabinetmaker, Jacob Siewers, and his apprentice. Siewers brought his other three apprentices three months later and stayed for several months. The Moravian influence is apparent in some of Day's pieces from that time.[43]

Day also owned a number of African Americans. Day owned fourteen slaves in 1850, which was more than was owned by 70 percent of North Carolinians who owned slaves (70 percent of North Carolinians owned none).[44] In his history of free African Americans in North Carolina, John Hope Franklin tells the stories of numerous other free African Americans who owned slaves mainly to free them, often their spouses or children. John Stanly, for example, a barber in New Bern, amassed a sizable fortune and purchased slaves in order to free them. Franklin notes that while Stanly "undoubtedly held some slaves with the view to increasing his wealth, he held others purely out of benevolence."[45] Stanly also took on a number of free African American children as apprentices to ensure that they would be working with someone they trusted.

Day seems not to have done the same. While the nature of his workshop meant that Day's slaves learned a trade and had a certain amount of liberty, Marshall and Leimenstoll note that "his slaves bore no family names that suggest a kinship tie to his family, his wife's family, or his mother's family" and argue that Day's slaves were purchased first and foremost as sources of wage-free labor.[46] Like many other antebellum professionals and politicians whose connections to slavery have been re-examined in recent years, Day's work is thus tainted by his profiteering from the slave system.[47]

White cabinetmaker John Swisegood also made a name for himself in the antebellum furniture industry. Born in 1796, Swisegood studied under the local cabinetmaker Mordecai Collins in Davidson County. From his shop in the same county, he produced two signed pieces and about forty others attributed to him. His signed furniture is two cherry and walnut tables crafted in the Federal style, which emphasizes clean lines, spare forms, and neoclassical decorations through finishes and paint instead of carvings.[48] According to some historians, Swisegood is also responsible for a number of unique, gothic headstones in Davidson County. These headstones, made of stone rather than wood, were never-theless a notable expression of the school's designs.[49]

Swisegood became known not only for his own pieces but for the school his work helped launch. This legacy was a product of the appren-tice system that sustained the furniture industry prior to the industrial period. Apprentices learned from the master artisan and incorporated elements of his artistic style into their own work, elements that were later discernible to collectors and furniture experts. The school Swise-good was associated with got underway with his predecessor Mordecai Collins and was continued by local cabinetmaker Jonathan Long after Swisegood moved to Illinois in 1848. Long's pieces preserve the gothic detailing that characterized the Swisegood headstones.

The late 1850s proved to be a turning point for the state's cabinetmak-ing industry, which was hit especially hard by the Panic of 1857. It was a luxury business sensitive to economic recessions. Hard economic times meant that more of a person's income went toward providing for the ne-cessities of life rather than expensive chairs and chests made from exotic woods. Less money from wealthy clients meant that many cabinetmak-ers experienced financial ruin. The Swisegood school ended in 1858 with Jonathan Long's death. Thomas Day also suffered financial deprivation. He stopped producing major pieces and died in 1861.

We can see the impact of the panic most clearly by comparing cabinetmaker numbers for 1850 with those of 1860. By 1860, the number of cabinetmakers in the state, according to Marshall and Leimenstoll, had decreased from 377 to 363. Both the area that formed the hub of the furniture belt and the counties that were home to the state's largest towns saw a decrease in the number of cabinetmakers, although cabinetmakers in the eastern counties of Craven and Pasquotank did not lose any cabinetmakers, and Chowan County managed to gain several.

These same patterns are seen in the 1860 census of manufacturers, which measured the number of industrial establishments that produced over $500 worth of goods. The number of such establishments rose only slightly from thirty-eight in 1850 to forty in 1860.[50] Of those forty, seventeen were located east of Orange County, and more than half of those were located in major eastern Piedmont and coastal towns. Counties such as Pitt and Nash lost all of their census-reported cabinetmaking businesses, while Cumberland and Rowan lost more than half. Future homes of the furniture industry such as Guilford, Caldwell, and Wilkes Counties had no furniture manufacturers large enough to be listed on the schedules for the census of manufacturers.

While it ended with the collapse of older cabinetmakers and artisanal schools, the late antebellum period brought a variety of technological and social advances to North Carolina that later proved vital to the modern furniture industry. After years of fits and starts, the state finally embraced railway transportation. The Wilmington and Weldon Railroad and the Raleigh and Gaston Railroad (both completed in 1840) were early ventures. In the 1850s, these two pioneers were joined by the Atlantic and North Carolina Railroad (completed 1858) and the Western North Carolina Railroad (partially completed by 1858) among others. North Carolina soon had a rail network that stretched from Morganton in the west to Morehead City in the east, with major lines going north into Virginia and south into South Carolina.[51]

These lines brought economic development to the previously isolated western parts of the state and helped rectify the backward nature of the state and its aversion to change. Civic boosters such as David Lowry

Swain and John Motley Morehead replaced for a time the agriculturally focused traditionalists in the school of Nathaniel Macon. Descendants of these boosters would lead the industrial awakening that the furniture industry would be part of at the end of the nineteenth century.

About the same time that these railroad lines were completed, the Civil War began. Both the war and its aftermath had a considerable impact on the fledgling cabinetmaking industry. Conflict plunged the state into economic despair that nearly halted the production of luxury goods entirely. Devastation from the war also adversely affected several eastern centers of cabinetmaking. Federal troops burned Elizabeth City and occupied New Bern, Fayetteville, and Raleigh. Railroads were damaged or completely destroyed at different times, the last being the Wilmington and Weldon, which the northern army severely damaged in the final weeks of the war. It took several years to rebuild these railroads.

The western part of the state was mostly spared from major conflict, although smaller clashes broke out in multiple towns. Stoneman's raid from late March through late April of 1865 resulted in sporadic damage throughout western North Carolina, including the present-day triad area. Raiders burned a depot along with cotton in High Point and a depot and several buildings in Statesville.[52] But there were fewer burnings and no battles to rival Bentonville or Plymouth in the east. Historian John G. Barrett notes that fierce Confederate resistance helped preserve the future furniture towns of Lexington and Thomasville from Stoneman's raiders.[53] In fact, the western Piedmont of North Carolina was the last sizable territory held by the Confederacy in the mid-Atlantic states at the end of the war. Jefferson Davis had his final cabinet meeting in Charlotte, while Joseph Johnston sent his troops home from one of the last unoccupied towns in the state, Greensboro.

The Civil War devastated the old economic and social system that had governed North Carolina for decades. Facing ruin, North Carolina was forced to adapt and to embrace industry to replace its old order. It would have to turn to its natural resources, transportation networks, and people to rebuild. In the New South that resulted from this process, the new furniture industry would play a pivotal role.

CHAPTER TWO

A Furniture Boom

HIGH POINT AND THE BEGINNINGS OF THE MODERN INDUSTRY, 1865–1900

After the Civil War, North Carolina found itself at a crossroads. Many of its railroads, towns, and finest homes lay in ruins, and approximately thirty-five thousand of its citizens had been killed.[1] Every cent of capital that had been tied up in the slave system vanished, and the state was forced to abandon the plantation system that had driven its economy since the eighteenth century. While much of the state's wealth remained tied up in agriculture, more attention was devoted with each passing year to the growth of industry. North Carolina would become an industrial state, first through tobacco and textiles and later through furniture, which gained a significant footing in the state in the last three decades of the nineteenth century.

Two movements helped develop the furniture industry in North Carolina. One was the growth of the modern northern furniture industry. The industry moved west from Boston and New England to New York in the mid-nineteenth century, and then its center shifted even further west, to Grand Rapids, Michigan, in the 1870s. Many of the same conditions favorable to the industry prevailed in Grand Rapids as in North Carolina: a large population to provide inexpensive labor, railroad connections, a local woodworking tradition, and vast stands of timber. Three companies (Berkey and Gay; Nelson, Matter; and Phoenix) dominated the industry and became some of the largest furniture companies in the country.[2]

Grand Rapids became a furniture mecca, producing a plethora of case goods, upholstered furniture, and chamber suites. The city's fame was predicated on its production of high-end pieces with the help of machinery. Machines in Grand Rapids furniture factories performed labor-saving tasks that allowed skilled personnel to craft specific joints and decorations by hand. As noted by Christian G. Carron, Grand Rapids' leading companies "probably reacted to the criticism of their making 'furniture with machinery' by adorning expensive furniture with handmade ornamentation," which "compensated for the coldness of largely machine-produced furniture by giving it warmth and individuality."[3] By 1901, the *White Directory of Manufacturers of Furniture and Kindred Goods* counted eighty-three firms in the city, more than half of the total for the entire state of North Carolina.[4]

The second movement that contributed to the growth of the furniture industry in North Carolina was the New South revival. Local boosters, working in concert with northern and sometimes foreign capital, started building railroads and factories wherever they could across the former Confederacy.[5] They took advantage of the South's plentiful resources and low wages to create vast riches that mainly went to northern sponsors and southern businessmen. Southern workers escaped isolation and grinding poverty, and the region started to build a middle class, at least for whites. In the span of a few decades, southern states had hundreds of railway miles, new economic sectors, and modern cities such as Charlotte, Atlanta, and Nashville.

North Carolina was a model New South state with growing cities and northern capital. Hundreds of miles of railway were built in the state between the 1860s and 1880s. Civic boosters such as Daniel Tompkins worked closely with company owners like the Holts and Dukes to build major factories and cities. North Carolina also elected business-friendly political leaders such as textile magnates Thomas Holt and Elias Carr, who both served as governor. Textiles and tobacco became statewide sources of prosperity in the New South period.

These two developments, the emergence of the modern furniture industry in the North and the New South openness to business growth, came together most notably in the Guilford County town of High Point. High Point was founded in 1859 as a community at the crossroads of the North Carolina Railroad and the Fayetteville and Western Plank Road, named for its position as the highest point on the railroad.[6] It had several small businesses such as hotels, general stores, and a drugstore in the

1860s.[7] Cabinetmakers worked both in and around the town throughout the antebellum period. By 1884, the town had a number of woodworking industries as well as cotton goods plants and several grist mills.[8] The first buildings in what is now known as the West High Street Historic District were completed before 1880.[9]

In the 1870s, William Henry Snow arrived in High Point with a business proposition. A Union captain from Vermont, Snow was familiar with the region's railroad connections, stands of lumber, and the woodworking traditions of the Quakers and Moravians who lived there. He also saw a market opportunity in the manufacture of shuttle blocks and bobbins for the growing textile industry. With these factors in mind, he started a lumber products company in 1871. Snow's business was successful, and he and his son Ernest Ansel Snow began to branch out, founding the Snow Lumber Company in 1881.

The Snows then took the next great leap for their business and region. Tradition has it that Ernest Ansel Snow grew frustrated at the use of his lumber products in furniture sold at inflated prices. Snow joined up with two local merchants, John H. Tate and Thomas Wrenn, and started the High Point Furniture Company in 1889. They relied on local labor and hired a factory superintendent from Charlotte to oversee the business.[10] Soon after founding the company, the original partners left to form their own businesses. The Tate Furniture Company and Snow's Eagle Furniture Company both opened in 1893, while Wrenn stayed to manage the original company with his brother Manleff J. Wrenn before moving to Marion in 1898.[11] These companies were enormously successful. Their affordable pieces were in high demand from the local textile industry. The railroads located in and near High Point could easily transport furniture to the textile mills of the Piedmont where they were needed in that region's new company towns.

The 1890s saw a number of fellow High Point businessmen follow the lead of Tate, Wrenn, and Snow. Alfred M. Rankin formed the Alma Furniture Company in 1895, and William Gaston Bradshaw founded the Globe Furniture Company in 1898.[12] These companies, along with several others, produced a variety of basic chairs, tables, and beds. Almost immediately, the companies were generating so many pieces that they were able to diversify. More specialized companies included the High Point Mantel and Table Company, the High Point Mattress and Bed Spring Company, the High Point Upholstering Company, and the National Lounge and Bed Spring Company.[13]

High Point in the 1890s was an archetypal boom town. Boom towns, like Manchester with textiles in the 1830s or Detroit with cars in the 1920s, witness a flurry of activity as one industry takes advantage of favorable market conditions and becomes enormously successful. High Point during this period was one of those towns. Its population more than doubled between 1880 and 1900. The number of furniture companies in the town went from nine in 1896 to twenty in 1900. The launching of new furniture businesses approached a frenzy. One story in the *High Point Enterprise* reported that "the late Frank Dalton . . . decided one morning that High Point needed a chair plant and that he walked out, called on a few friends and thereupon in an hour or so the Southern Chair Company was a realization."[14]

These factories were rudimentary and produced cheap furniture that appealed to textile towns. A comparison of the 1901 catalog of a High Point firm, the High Point Furniture Company, with that of a contemporary Grand Rapids furniture company, Bishop Furniture Company, shows a marked contrast. The High Point company's catalog listed fifty-four pieces at an average of $8 per piece.[15] Prices ranged from a poplar single bed at $0.65 to an oak suite priced at $30. The average price of the furniture listed in the Grand Rapids company's catalog, by contrast, was approximately $21, and a three-piece bedroom suite went for as much as $79.75.[16] And these prices were modest: According to a circa-1900 list from leading firm Berkey and Gay, prices ranged from $10 for a rattan chair to $300 for a mahogany bed and bureau.[17]

In the early years, much furniture manufacturing was still done by hand. Joiners, planers, and assemblers worked alongside rudimentary woodworking machines and paid attention to each piece. There were no conveyor belts, Ford-style assembly lines, or massive machines to rival the setup of the textile industry. Some furniture factories did not manufacture any parts directly from lumber. For instance, in its early years the Tomlinson Chair Manufacturing Company simply pieced together chairs from parts shipped in from the North.

A 1902 map of High Point created for the purpose of determining fire insurance liability indicates the limited use of machinery in the early years of the furniture industry. Two furniture-related factories, the Tomlinson Chair Manufacturing Company and the High Point Mattress and Bed Spring Company, listed "hand" as a major source of power.[18] The rest had woodworking machines that were powered mostly by the burning of refuse and scrap wood. When companies ran out of wood scraps, they could purchase coal from local merchants.[19] Nearly every factory on the map used Sturtevant fans, a type of fan that blew shavings from the woodworking area into the boiler and produced steam.[20] The machines that this process powered were not much more advanced than those powered by Thomas Day's six-horsepower steam engine a half century before. Limited machinery meant furniture companies did not require much in the way of capital, and therefore it was fairly easy for new companies to enter the field. It was one of the reasons why the state's furniture industry could boast that it did not require northern or British capital like many textile and other manufacturers in the New South.

Along with the factories themselves, High Point also built a business infrastructure that would allow its furniture industry to continue to grow. By 1903, the town had three bank branches, an insurance agency, three machine shops, a telephone exchange, and municipally run water works, lights, and sewage systems.[21] A key development in its industrial growth was the foundation of the *High Point Enterprise* in 1881 under editor G. F. Crutchfield. Crutchfield's successor, J. J. Farriss, was a booster in the vein of Henry Grady in Atlanta or Daniel Tompkins in Charlotte.

Farriss wrote a series of pamphlets beginning in 1896 that touted the city's progress and profiled many of its business leaders. In the first, Farriss stressed his impartiality and his reason for creating the pamphlets, noting that "there is no Land Company or Boom back of this work. It is simply the observations of one who has watched the phenomenal growth of a North Carolina Manufacturing City, and who is impelled by a sense of duty as well as pleasure to let other people know it."[22]

Farriss went on to describe an idealized High Point. High Point's growth as an industrial town, he believed, owed to its forward-looking citizens. They formed a town that "believes in home and hospitality—patronizes home enterprises and never objects to newcomers sharing its hospitality."[23] They were "progressive and conservative," open minded but also notably sober and responsible. Likely in order to emphasize a contrast between High Point and textile towns, Farriss also noted that most of the workingmen of High Point owned their own homes, and further, that instead of relying on northern or foreign banks, "factories have all been built by home capital" and that "as soon as the people get enough surplus in hand another factory goes up, as a matter of course."[24]

High Point's growth attracted attention as early as the 1890s. An account of the furniture industry published in the *Durham Globe* in 1892 described a city that was "in it for business; in it for her advantage, and is a rushing, booming town." The profile mainly focused on the city's longer-established industries but also mentioned the High Point Furniture Company, identifying it as "one of the solid institutions of the place" and characterizing it as a company that "manufacture[s] medium and cheap grade furniture, and they give universal satisfaction." The *Globe* article's overall assessment of High Point was that it was a city primed for growth: "For the most part her business men are progressive and aggressive, and there is no doubt about the future of the place."[25] This appraisal was confirmed by a short account in the *Semi-Weekly Messenger* of Wilmington that referred to High Point as "the center of the furniture industry in the south."[26]

In 1901, another glowing review of High Point's growth and development appeared in several southern newspapers. This review summarized a rosy report by one E. M. Armstrong on the furniture industry in his hometown: "It would be tedious to mention the name of the different factories and their managers and the various articles of furniture manufactured, which include everything that is needed for use and ornament in a modern dwelling, business, house or office. These goods are shipped to every State of the Union and to some foreign countries."[27] According to Armstrong, the plants were profitable and beneficial to the town, bringing in much-needed income while also providing work that was not particularly degrading.

Armstrong also documented the financial success of the plants, noted that most of the stockholders were local, and described the racial makeup of the labor force: "All labor employed is white with the exception of a few negroes who drive drays and handle lumber around the yards." This segregation was often mentioned in literature designed to persuade new white employees to move to textile and furniture-making areas. Indeed, many of the plants in areas with large numbers of African Americans, such as the plant in Martin County, failed relatively early. The White Furniture Company was an exception to the all-white makeup of most plants; it had six African Americans on its forty-five-employee workforce in 1898, one of whom operated a machine.[28] Women were also excluded almost entirely from the industry at this early stage. The male-dominated sphere of the furniture industry, which also hired children, contrasted with the textile industry, which hired a significant number of women in its early years.[29]

The work of Farriss, Armstrong, and other boosters ignored the limitations of furniture-related prosperity for the people of High Point. Despite its localized nature and better conditions compared with the textile industry, the furniture industry was still a New South industry devoted to the maximization of profit and the building of wealth for its leaders. Little of that wealth reached the workers. Initial wages offered by furniture companies in High Point were much lower than those paid by their northern counterparts. The average furniture wage varied depending on year and factory, but throughout the 1890s most High Point factories reported daily wages of less than $1.50. Wages reported from 1890 to 1897 were less than the average manufacturing wage for the county. In 1897, the average furniture wage was 97.5 cents for men and 42.5 cents for children per day, significantly less than northern or midwestern furniture wages but more than the 65 cents per day textile workers earned.[30]

The leaders of the furniture industry in North Carolina were aware of labor conditions in northern and midwestern cities and knew that the lower wages paid in their region gave them a competitive advantage. An 1890 report by the North Carolina Bureau of Labor Statistics took up the question of wages. When asked to comment on his business, the owner of a door, sash, blind, and furniture factory in Gaston County said that "the increase of the necessary expenses, in the way of living, for our hands requires an increase of wages, but the low prices for our manufactured goods, and the competition we have to contend with, will not allow us to increase the wages of the hands, but has rather an opposite tendency, or operate with cheaper labor."[31]

Several other early factories were located in the western part of the state. One of the first factories in North Carolina, the Furniture Manufacturing Company in Old Fort, was incorporated in 1879 and advertised in the early 1880s, although it was likely defunct by 1885.[32] Avery and Erwin in Asheville and the Lenoir Furniture Company in Lenoir were, like the furniture companies in High Point, near timber stands and railroad lines. Avery and Erwin, founded by at least 1886 and renamed Skyland Furniture in 1895, was a manufacturer of "medium grade chamber suits and bedsteads," while Lenoir, founded in 1889, produced inexpensive furniture. (George Alexander Bernhardt, a descendant of Lenoir's first president, J. M. Bernhardt, is a leader of the furniture industry today.)[33] Other factories opened in the 1880s and 1890s in Charlotte, Asheboro, and Ramseur.

Goldsboro Manufacturing Company in Goldsboro was unique as an early eastern furniture factory. It was incorporated in 1887 and by 1897 was producing medium- and high-grade chamber suites.[34] Herman Weil, one of the city's leading businessmen, was an early owner.[35] Like many of its western counterparts, the Goldsboro plant was located next to large stands of timber and a sizable river, the Neuse River, which could provide power and help with transportation. It was also near the North Carolina Railroad, which allowed transportation to a variety of tobacco and textile towns. An 1890 report in the Raleigh *State Chronicle* stated that the company produced furniture made of sweetgum wood that was "being shipped in large quantities abroad, and find[ing] a ready sale in the home market."[36] In 1900, a local report noted that the factory had two million board feet of timber on its yard, a 150-horsepower engine for its wood-working machines, and a capable superintendent who brought with him twenty years of experience from Grand Rapids.[37]

Goldsboro itself was a sizable tobacco and textile town with 5,847 people in 1900, 1,600 more people than High Point and seven times the population of Thomasville at that time. Its furniture industry may have inspired other easterners such as a New Bern carpenter who wrote to the Bureau of Labor and Printing in 1895 to make a case for establishing furniture factories in his region. Furniture, he claimed, "can be manufactured here much cheaper than at any point I know of, as the cost of labor and material is so cheap."[38] Nevertheless, even though the Goldsboro Manufacturing Company (renamed Kemp Furniture Company in 1931) prospered, it remained one of the few furniture factories in the eastern part of the state for decades.

Many of the early factories outside of High Point met with varying degrees of success. Plants in Mebane, Goldsboro, and Dunn lasted for decades. Skyland Furniture in Asheville closed in 1897, while Elliott and Marsh in Charlotte closed in 1899 and Alberta Chair Company in Ramseur closed in 1908.[39] Beginnings in Lenoir were inauspicious as well. The first plant in Lenoir failed in 1897, and its immediate successor filed for bankruptcy two years later.[40] Although success varied, none of these early factories started a boom like that in High Point.

Thomasville and Lexington, two later centers of furniture manufacturing, were also building the foundations for their furniture sectors at this time. Thomasville, founded in 1852, was located on the North Carolina Railroad and was close to numerous cabinetmakers in Davidson County. There is record of a chair plant in Thomasville as early as 1865, although that reference may have been to a chair-producing artisanal shop.[41] The more notable Standard Chair Company was founded in 1898 by John Lambeth, Frank Lambeth, E. W. Cates, and John Pope. By 1901, the town had five furniture factories.[42] Lexington, the county seat of Davidson County, also had three factories by 1901 and was transforming into a center for furniture production.[43]

Arguably the earliest furniture factory in North Carolina did not follow the High Point model in any way. David and William White founded the White Furniture Company in 1881 in the small Alamance County town of Mebane. Their sizable factory, located on the North Carolina Railroad like many others, was rebuilt in 1923 after a fire and still stands as renovated apartments today. Unlike High Point companies, White Furniture's approach was to make the best pieces, sometimes out of exotic woods, and to advertise those pieces in northern and western markets familiar with high-quality furniture.[44] This approach is illustrated by an 1886 letter written by William White in which he advertised the company's "strictly first-class selected work" and noted that "we have seen in the short time we have been in the business, that to take bills so low that we have to use cheap lumber, is not the way to build up a trade."[45]

White Furniture's quality-focused mindset is reflected in a price list from 1910. While the High Point Furniture Company catalog's average price would have been approximately $9.15 in 1914, White Furniture's products went for an average of $15.10 that same year.[46] White Furniture also offered more variety than its fellow North Carolina companies. While companies such as High Point Furniture and Eagle Furniture offered most of their pieces in only poplar or oak, White Furniture offered oak, American walnut, circular walnut, and mahogany as well as a dull or polished finish.[47]

By 1900, the North Carolina furniture industry was not yet the behemoth it would become over the next three decades. There were still only 44 establishments classified as "furniture, factory product" in the state in the 1900 census, compared with approximately 177 factories producing cotton goods and approximately 100 making tobacco-related products.[48] Furniture factories were small and closely associated with the textile industry. Cabinetmakers were still responsible for a sizable portion of the furniture output in North Carolina, with the 1901 *White Directory* listing sixteen firms specifically identified as cabinetmakers. But the rapid growth in High Point made its mark. Observers and entrepreneurs saw the new factories springing up overnight, along with the new businesses and the stately homes being built almost daily on High and Main Streets.

They were aware of economic opportunity and the possibility that the High Point experience could be duplicated in numerous other places in the Piedmont and mountain regions. It was only a matter of time before the North Carolina furniture industry would take its proper place as a key part of the state's economy.

CHAPTER THREE

Growth and Expansion

THE NORTH CAROLINA FURNITURE
INDUSTRY, 1900–1920

In 1900, the North Carolina furniture industry was still relatively small. It produced $1.5 million worth of goods and was the state's seventh largest industry according to the 1900 census, only barely edging out the fertilizer and leather businesses.[1] More than half of the state's forty-four furniture manufacturers were in High Point.[2] Beaufort representative John H. Small, in a 1902 speech on the state's economy, conceded that "the magnitude of the industry is not such, perhaps, as would attract general attention."[3] But over the following two decades, through economic development and the work of pioneering industrialists, the furniture industry would assume its role with textiles and tobacco as one of the state's twentieth-century economic engines.

The 1900s and 1910s saw a continuation in High Point of the phenomenal growth that had characterized furniture manufacturing during the previous two decades. New plants continued to be built at nearly the same rate as they had been in the last decade of the nineteenth century. Some grew out of earlier companies, such as the Myrtle Desk Company, which was started by a founder of the older Alma Furniture Company.[4] There were also several consolidations. The Globe Furniture Company (founded 1896) and the Home Furniture Company (founded 1890) merged in 1902.[5] The Kearns Furniture Company, one of the most successful in the town, was formed in 1904 by a merger of the High Point Mantel and Table Company and a plant of the American Lumber Company.[6]

Despite these consolidations, the average factory plant remained small throughout the first half of the twentieth century. The 1920 census noted that 53 percent of the state's furniture plants produced between

$100,000 and $500,000 worth of goods.[7] There were only three plants that produced more than $1 million worth of goods. By comparison, 61 percent of cotton goods plants produced more than $500,000 worth of goods, and eighty-five plants produced over $1 million worth of goods. While the textile industry was the state's largest industry and was much larger than the furniture industry, smaller industries were also more concentrated. The fertilizer industry had a quarter of the establishments of the furniture industry, yet it had eleven plants producing more than $1 million worth of goods. Even the flour mill industry, which employed fewer than a thousand people compared with the furniture industry's seventy nine hundred, had more million-dollar plants.

These statistics are surprising at first glance. In much of the nation's industry, concentration and the formation of trusts were the order of the day. Larger companies in fields such as steel, oil, and railroads could command cheaper material and transportation costs. The Standard Oil, U.S. Steel, and American Tobacco trusts created some of the largest companies and the most sizable fortunes the nation had ever seen. But with furniture, the main costs came from labor. There was simply no need to take over a supply line when the factory was located near a stand of trees and a dozen eager lumber companies. The industry also had no significant barriers of entry. There were no pipelines, large stores of electricity, or complex technical knowledge required to start a furniture factory. Therefore, many people did so throughout the state, and the larger companies had so much demand that they saw no need to swallow up their competitors.[8]

There were around twenty-six furniture factories in High Point in 1904, a number that grew to about thirty-five in 1916.[9] The town's population grew over 300 percent in the first twenty years of the twentieth century, making it the state's eighth largest town by 1920.[10] New banks were built and furniture magnates started new businesses. These businessmen constructed some of the city's finest homes, such as the sixty-two-hundred-square-foot Fraser-Wilson House (1905) and the imposing Kirkman House (1900), both colonial revival structures located on West High Street.[11] It was around 1900 that the town first gained the nickname "Grand Rapids of the South," a comparison to what was then the country's leading furniture-producing city.[12]

Many of the furniture companies in High Point continued to focus on the cheap and medium-grade furniture that had originally fueled the furniture boom in the 1890s. Others attempted to diversify their product lines. The Continental Furniture Company, founded in 1902 by Fred N. Tate, focused on more expensive pieces than its competitors, including "fine grade chamber suits, sideboards, ward-robes and chiffoniers." In order to produce these more expensive pieces, a pamphlet from the period noted, "the company employs a large force of skilled mechanics, who manufacture some beautiful creations in furniture."[13]

Companies expanded in the 1900s beyond the construction of simple wooden furniture into related furniture fields. The High Point Metallic Bed Company, organized by furniture pioneer Manleff J. Wrenn and others, ventured into metallurgy and ironwork.[14] A mirror company was founded in 1904 along with a branch of the Pittsburgh Plate Glass Company in 1905, both of which produced pieces for cabinets and sideboards. Several veneer companies also sprang up. Veneering, the practice of gluing on a thin strip of luxury wood such as mahogany or walnut to a cheaper core, was common with cabinetmakers at all levels of quality but was particularly helpful for the more affordable markets that High Point focused on.[15]

Greater complexity of materials and designs required more expertise. The furniture industry could no longer simply improvise, relying only on local employees and a few experts temporarily shipped in. The city's industry leaders therefore sought out talent from outside. The branch of the glass company from Pittsburgh was joined by the High Point Glass and Decorative Company, founded by A. W. Klemme, a trained stained glass artisan from Cincinnati.[16] In 1902, Philadelphia native Joel A. Blair built a metallic bed factory.[17]

Furniture companies and economic growth created fertile ground for the cultivation of local and state leaders. Chief among these was J. Elwood Cox. Born in Northampton County in 1856, Cox moved to High Point in 1880 and soon took over William Henry Snow's lumber products business. His success at expanding that company led him to a wide variety of other positions, including founder of the Globe Furniture Company and later president of the consolidated Globe-Home Furniture Company.[18] He also started moving up the ladder of Republican politics in Guilford County.[19]

In 1908, Cox gained renown when he ran for governor as the Republican candidate. He was described by the Republican *Times-Mercury* of Hickory as a "quiet and dignified" man and as "a business man" about whom there was nothing "to suggest the politician."[20] Cox's nomination was part of a concerted effort by Republicans to embrace business magnates and mill leaders in that year's election.[21] To that end, Cox also received the support of the then-nascent furniture industry. Republican newspapers circulated a letter signed by High Point's furniture leaders noting that J. Elwood Cox was a friend to labor and had "spent his life" advocating for manufacturing and the city.[22] Fred Tate, W. P. Ragan, and Charles F. Tomlinson spoke glowingly of Cox at a rally following the candidate's nomination, with Tomlinson calling him "the Governor of High Point."[23] Several of these men were Democrats and so did not support him fully. But Sam White of White Furniture Company did. In a February 1908 letter to Cox, White wrote that "the good of the state" required him to run and that his victory would bring the state "in the lime light of the country." White concluded his clearly pro-Republican letter by stating that "I honestly believe that you can and will be elected. If I were a betting man, I'd gamble on it."[24]

In the 1898 and 1900 state campaigns the Democrats used violence and intimidation to discourage voters from voting for Republicans and Populists. In 1898, they even staged a coup d'état of the local "fusionist" government in Wilmington, a collaboration between the Populist Party and the Republican Party. The result of these tactics was a constitutional amendment barring nearly all African Americans and many poor whites from voting. In addition to its long-term role in solidifying white dominance and ushering in the Jim Crow era, these tactics in the 1898 and 1900 campaigns paved the way for future candidates having to prove their "commitment" to white supremacy. In the 1908 campaign, Democrats portrayed Cox as moderate on the question of race, even though his party had purged African Americans several years before. Democrats declared that instead of fighting in the white supremacy campaigns of 1898 and 1900 he was "then too busy with his bobbin trust."[25] Cox ended up losing by 37,342 votes, which made him the most successful Republican candidate in the state during the first seventy years of the twentieth century.[26] Even though he lost, Cox's run helped bolster the Republicans in the state. It also showed the strength of High Point and the furniture industry on the state level. In that way, Cox's run was similar to the earlier ascendancy of Democratic textile magnate Thomas Holt, who became governor in 1890.

The Cox campaign symbolized the arrival of the furniture industry in North Carolina's political consciousness. In 1903, only a year after John H. Small's remarks about the small size of the industry, Governor Charles Brantley Aycock gave a speech in Greensboro in which he stated that "within this county the forty furniture factories, giving employment to thousands of skilled laborers, sell their furniture in Grand Rapids, and take tribute to their superior workmanship from every State in the Union."[27] By 1904, Aycock was able to say that "other industries, notably the manufacture of furniture and other articles of wood, have fully kept pace, if not outstript that of cotton manufacturing."[28]

Outside of the political realm, other leaders of the industry included the brothers Sidney H. and Charles F. Tomlinson, whose family had lived in Guilford County since the eighteenth century. Sidney began the Tomlinson Chair Manufacturing Company in 1900 on a prime spot of land right on the Southern Railway. Taking advantage of local cheap labor, the company pieced together chairs made out of parts manufactured in New England. It was enormously successful, and two plant additions were built between 1906 and 1911.

In 1911, the Tomlinson Chair Manufacturing Company made what was then the largest purchase of the state's furniture industry when it bought the Globe-Home Furniture Company. This consolidation combined the South's largest chair manufacturer with its largest furniture manufacturer in what was described by the *Wilmington Morning*

Star as "one of the biggest things ever—in High Point's manufacturing world."[29] Following the merger, Tomlinson Chair continued to introduce new innovations to the furniture field. One of the most influential was the matching dining-room sets and living room suites the company marketed in 1916, an idea that would soon be copied by Tomlinson's competitors.[30]

High Point's earliest competitors in the field met with differing fates as the twentieth century progressed. Nineteenth-century plants in Northampton County, Martin County, and Cumberland County had all closed by 1920.[31] White Furniture Company in Mebane, one of the oldest in the state, continued to thrive, however, and its reputation for fine pieces grew throughout the late nineteenth century. The company received a national boost in prestige when it was commissioned by the military to produce furniture for personnel working on the Panama Canal.[32] White Furniture also received the furniture contract for the Grove Park Inn in Asheville, one of the state's most prestigious hotels. The company's furniture can still be found in that hotel's rooms.[33] The White Furniture factory was joined by two other furniture companies in Mebane by 1920.

Another exceptional early furniture center was Thomasville, the small town that most closely matched High Point's growth. Following a lull in the late nineteenth century, the town received a boost when Thomas Jefferson Finch bought the struggling Thomasville Chair Company in 1907. Finch had moved to Thomasville from Randolph County ten years before and started a general store. These businesses gave the city the infrastructure to support a growing furniture industry. Finch bought three more furniture companies by 1910. His sons, most notably Thomas Finch Jr., joined the company over the next decade and created a furniture dynasty. Thomasville had at least eleven furniture manufacturing plants by 1916, according to a business directory.[34] By the 1920 census, Thomasville was the twenty-second-largest town in the state.[35]

The successes of High Point and Thomasville gave rise to a furniture-producing region in North Carolina. This so-called furniture belt, known in the 1950s and 1960s as the "furniture figure eight" on account of the network of highways centered in Iredell County that linked furniture-producing towns, comprised much of the western Piedmont as well as the foothills region from High Point west to Morganton. The furniture figure eight was similar to the textile ministate described by Brent Glass, a region from the Haw River valley in the east to the foothills in the west that "consisted of a series of mills and mill villages linked by railroads and a publicly financed highway system" and that was backed by electric power and banking prowess from Charlotte.[36]

A parallel story to the rise of the furniture industry in the western Piedmont was the long-term stagnation of plants in the east. Eastern North Carolina had timber stands like those in the west and a robust timber industry in areas such as Martin, Bertie, and Halifax Counties. There were also a few furniture factories in such places as New Bern, Dunn, and Wilmington in addition to Goldsboro. Close by in the central Piedmont, Raleigh had two factories while Durham and Sanford had one.[37] The Dunn plant, Newberry Brothers and Cowell, founded before 1902, was particularly successful.[38] But it is telling that by 1920, no eastern town had more than two furniture factories. There was simply too much competition in the eastern counties from agriculture, textiles, and tobacco for furniture plants to flourish.

Development in the foothills was particularly significant. In the early twentieth century, the region was primed for furniture development just as the western Piedmont had been in earlier decades. Major railroads such as the Southern Railway and the Carolina and Northwestern Railway were expanding their lines.[39] Railroads helped facilitate the growth of the lumber industry, which took advantage of unbroken forests even more expansive than those in Guilford and Davidson Counties. Large numbers of local men needed work, and there were a number of entrepreneurs. Local towns in the region were also becoming centers for the textile industry, which created demand for cheap to medium-grade furniture in mill homes. By 1902, many of the counties that would later become centers for the furniture industry had cotton mills; in 1905, Catawba County was fourth in the number of cotton mills of any county in the state.[40]

One of the most impressive of these new foothills furniture towns was Drexel, located in central Burke County near the county seat of Morganton. Located at the intersection of a wagon road and the Southern Railway, Drexel originated at the site of a factory that produced lumber for corn cribs. In 1903, four local businessmen came together to form a furniture company with $75,000 worth of stock.[41] The Drexel Furniture Company produced cheap furniture in the High Point vein in its early years, sometimes of questionable quality. As relayed in the official history of Drexel Enterprises written in 1963, one of its products was "a three-piece suite of solid oak-bureau, washstand and bed, which sold for $14.50 wholesale. One dealer admitted that he was sometimes tempted to sell the packing case and throw the furniture away."[42]

The Drexel Furniture Company's early years were full of challenges. Machinery was rudimentary and liable to failure, and capital was hard to come by. The factory suffered a catastrophic fire in 1908 that required the complex to be rebuilt. But the amount of furniture it sold continued to grow. Eventually, Drexel became a stable, successful company. Ten years after the 1908 fire, Drexel was able to expand its plant and purchase the Blue Ridge Furniture Company in Marion.[43]

Marion, the county seat of McDowell County, was located approximately thirty miles east of Asheville. It was a sleepy railroad town of about a thousand people when High Point magnate Thomas F. Wrenn arrived in 1896. Wrenn immediately went to work building a new furniture plant, the Catawba Furniture Company, which soon focused on producing chamber suites.[44] Marion had four furniture factories and a veneer plant by 1916.[45] By 1920, the town's population had nearly doubled from its 1890 level. The town also had two hotels, several textile and hosiery mills, and a Dodge garage by that year, and by 1922 it had two banks.[46]

Another of High Point's eventual rivals in the furniture field emerged from humble beginnings in the early twentieth century. Hickory was much larger than Marion, Thomasville, or Drexel in 1900, having 2,535 residents according to the census.[47] Its growth stemmed from the railroad, which was routed through the community of Hickory Tavern when the Western North Carolina Railroad came in the late 1850s.[48] The town's first two furniture factories opened in 1901, according to a July 24, 1901, article published in the *Times-Mercury*. The first, known as the Hickory Furniture Company, was started by local citizens, while the second was opened by Thomas J. Martin of Chester, South Carolina, an entrepreneur who had already succeeded in the cotton seed oil business.[49] By that time, Hickory also had a full complement of other businesses: foundries, a large wagon company, a bottling plant, three hotels, and a bank.[50]

The Hickory and Martin furniture companies fulfilled large orders from their factories in eastern Hickory throughout the early twentieth century. But with the exception of a third factory for chairs that opened in 1911, they remained the only furniture factories in the town for several years.[51] Hickory was prosperous and becoming a furniture hub, but it did not match the prodigious growth of new centers like High Point. Other leading furniture towns included Statesville, North Wilkesboro, Morganton, Lenoir, and Lexington. By the early 1900s, the North Carolina furniture industry employed a substantial number of people. The leading furniture towns all had their first factories by 1910, a year in which over six thousand people were employed in making furniture and iceboxes according to that year's census.[52]

Large cities also began to play a role in the furniture industry during this time. These cities had abundant capital and space along railroads to facilitate the growth of furniture factories. Greensboro and Winston-Salem each had a considerable furniture sector by 1920.[53] Greensboro had one of the state's first furniture factories, the Greensboro Furniture Company, which opened in 1890. This factory followed the High Point model of offering low-cost furniture, sometimes at a lower cost than many of its High Point rivals. While the Greensboro Furniture Company closed in 1915, by 1922 three furniture factories, three furniture repair businesses, and fifteen furniture dealers were in operation in the city.[54]

Winston-Salem's furniture industry was slightly larger. It had three factories as well as four repair businesses and eighteen furniture dealers by 1921.[55] A 1920 article in the *Winston-Salem Journal* proclaimed that the city was the second largest furniture center in the South by output behind High Point.[56] But the industry was not nearly large enough to compete with the primary industries in those cities. Therefore, Greensboro and Winston-Salem went on to mainly focus on tobacco and textiles, although a good number of their remaining businesses were associated with furniture.

Companies began to have an impact on the social fabric of the Piedmont in the first two decades of the twentieth century, mainly in the way they fostered the growth of established towns. Most of these furniture factories were located along the railroads in downtown areas. The workers lived nearby, sometimes in houses that they owned. Their experience was different from that of textile mill workers, who lived in tight-knit communities and who were forced to depend on the factory store. The furniture workforce was part of the town, rather than off in its own mill village, leading to greater growth for incorporated towns that had multiple industries.

The different power sources that furniture and textile factories relied on contributed to their different locations. The textile industry had originally formed in isolated mill villages along the waterways of the Piedmont. These cotton mills mainly used waterpower. According to the 1920 census, more than 10 percent of the total of the textile mills' power (twenty-seven thousand horsepower) was generated by water. Conversely, since it never had a rural connection to waterways, the furniture industry relied more on coal and wood scraps for power throughout the early twentieth century, with only 0.2 percent of its power coming from water in 1920. Because the furniture industry was centered in towns, it also came to be dependent on steam power for lighting.

Another difference between the textile and furniture industries was how the workers were paid. One of the most objectionable aspects of life in company towns, both in North Carolina and elsewhere, was pay in scrip. As Hall and coauthors in *Like a Family* note, the checks issued by the scrip system were often worthless and the debt that resulted from low pay was similar to eviction, "a heavy-handed and often counterproductive instrument of control that left workers feeling 'as if they are enslaved.'"[57] The furniture industry, by contrast, was known for paying in cash, or as Bill Bamberger and Cathy Davidson put it, the furniture industry offered "actual cash money for actual labor."[58]

The communities that furniture employees lived in varied considerably. Factories in 1920 stretched from communities as small as Denton and Edwards Crossroads and cities as large as Charlotte and Greensboro.[59] While companies owned a number of homes that they rented to employees, many workers in High Point owned their house.[60] Lewis Hine, famous for his photographs of child labor, worked for the Works Progress Administration in the 1930s photographing laborers and companies throughout the country. He took pictures of worker housing near Tomlinson of High Point that show rows of houses of varying size and quality located within sight of the factory and the downtown area. Hine also took photographs of lower-quality housing for African American employees of both local furniture and textile mills, which he labeled "hovels."[61] He did not, however, take any photographs of child laborers at furniture factories in High Point but instead focused on child labor in the textile industry.

A division among tasks was introduced early on within furniture factories. Jobs, which included joining, finishing, upholstering, and painting, ranged with respect to the level of skill required and the level of reliance on machinery depending on the type and quality level of furniture being produced.[62] But the era of apprenticeships for furniture work was over, and employees were given the most strenuous and complex tasks in the factory after limited training.

Although apprenticeships were out of fashion by the late nineteenth century, child labor was not. The children in the plants often did the same jobs as adult employees. Children were exposed to harsh fumes, dust, and rough or unsafe working conditions. A set of Lewis Hine photographs of child furniture laborers outside of North Carolina showed children who tied bed springs and sawed lumber. One of Lewis's captions references a boy who nearly lost his arms pushing wood into a circular saw.[63] E. Leroy Briggs, a successful consultant in the furniture industry, recalled working at the age of thirteen in a lumber yard: "In those days the handling of lumber was plank by plank, by hand. We stacked the boards on pallets-movable rail-mounted pallets. The lumber came to us by motor truck from a lumber area around High Point—most of it in fact was from up in Virginia. The logger's trucks came and dumped the planks off and we had to pick them up one by one, stack them on pallets and we rolled them on rails around the yard. . . . It was pretty splintery, rough lumber, and gloves didn't do a bit of good because a pair of gloves, in that use, wouldn't last a day. We just did it bare-handed, and we had two or three break times for coffee and for lunch, and that was when we sat and picked the splinters out of our hands."[64]

Another furniture executive, J. Wade Kincaid of Kincaid Furniture, worked for a High Point furniture factory at the age of twelve during the 1920s. He had the position of "drawer boy," which meant he was in charge of making drawers and fitting them into case goods. In a 1988 interview, Kincaid recalled the long hours, low pay, and harmful conditions. He remembered the dust particulates and the varnish fumes of the era and said that he and the other employees "wore coverings over our faces and something over our heads, mouths and noses to keep from breathing that stuff."[65]

The number of children in the industry was much smaller than that in textile mills (5.9%) and knit goods (11.9%). But children were still an integral part of the furniture labor force. In a 1902 letter to the state Bureau of Labor Statistics, White Furniture Company secretary-treasurer J. S. White defended the practice. He wrote, "We are not troubled, as in the cotton mills, with the loafing, drinking father; so in some cases there should be allowed discretion on the part of the superintendent about hiring child help. The work these little boys do is very light, not at all irksome, plenty of light, no dust in our plant, and they cannot only be earning something but as well be a training to their young minds and keep them from idleness."[66]

In 1919, Congress passed a law imposing an extra tax on companies that employed a child. Drexel Furniture Company was charged the tax and sued. The case went all the way to the Supreme Court. In the majority opinion in *Bailey v. Drexel Furniture Company*, William Howard Taft, former president turned chief justice, ruled that the tax was unconstitutional because its primary purpose was to penalize and regulate companies. It was one of many *Lochner*-era court cases that struck down federal regulations regarding workers, and it contributed to another decade-plus of child labor throughout the country. While child labor was eventually banned in the 1930s, the *Bailey* case was cited again as recently as 2012, when it was fully reversed by the Roberts court in its decision to let the Affordable Care Act stand.[67]

Most of the employees performing joining, finishing, upholstering, and painting tasks were men. Only 3.3 percent of furniture factory workers in 1920 were female, and 2.1 percent of that number were girls under sixteen years of age.[68] Furthermore, they were overwhelmingly white. Less than 7 percent of operatives (employees who worked on machines) in the industry were African American according to the 1930 census, the earliest census to track that percentage.[69] Indeed, as we have seen, the predominantly white workforce was a selling point in the Jim Crow South. A *Greensboro Daily News* article from 1915 praising the progress of the industry quoted two factory owners who boasted that "the employees of their mills are almost all native whites."[70] African Americans who did work for the factory were still limited to demanding physical jobs such as hauling lumber outside of the factory.

The mid-to-late 1910s were a challenging stretch for the furniture industry. A number of plants closed or were forced into bankruptcy. These included the Columbia Furniture Company (1913), the Greensboro Furniture Company (1915), and the Craven Brothers Furniture Company (1916).[71] This pressure was a result of the cyclical nature of boom industries like North Carolina furniture. Recessions meant less disposable income and a consequent drop in the amount of money spent on furniture by the public.

The low barriers to entering the furniture industry also led to frequent turnover and closings. Because it was relatively easy to open a factory but hard to run it properly, many factory owners, lacking experience, became overwhelmed. They did not know how to secure lines of credit, establish supplier relationships, or make the other connections that a twentieth-century business required. Grocers and merchants continued to open factories, but now these companies had to compete with larger concerns that had cornered a large share of the furniture market already. Businessmen overextended their credit, declared bankruptcy, and sold off their assets in fire sales. Each closing meant lost economic activity and up to a few dozen unemployed workers.

The First World War also had an impact on the industry's development. All across the country factories turned to the production of armaments and materials directly connected to the war effort. Textile mills thrived because they were able to produce uniforms and articles of clothing related to the war effort, but furniture did not have the same ready application. The war caused a general economic downturn and led to a severe labor shortage. Home building declined, which decreased demand for new furniture, and fuel shortages led to plant shutdowns.[72] The still nascent Southern Furniture Market was canceled during the war years, preventing it from gaining much regional or national traction.

This stress was still evident by 1920. As a writer for the *Dispatch* of Lexington noted that year, "Manufacturing in this county has felt the depression to the largest extent, this being particularly true of the furniture industry. While a certain amount of furniture is a necessity[,] much of it is classed as a luxury. . . . [O]ne furniture man in this section is reported to have spent a week recently in New York state and did not sell a piece of goods, although having $150,000 worth stored away in the warehouses at his factory."[73]

The war period also witnessed a significant increase in labor unrest in the furniture industry. Prior to 1918, furniture boosters prided themselves on the relatively cordial relations between workers and employers in the industry. As J. J. Farriss argued in 1915, "Those who come South to engage in the manufacturing business first ask about the labor problem. There is no problem here. Labor as a rule receives a just return for services rendered and as a rule it may be said that there is no unrest or uneasy feeling among either the employer or employee. The aggregate amount of wages received by an operative is not so large as in Michigan, but the net profit that accrues to the laborer is equally as much if not more."[74] Farriss was a booster for High Point who clearly took the side of management in any labor dispute. But even the labor-friendly press agreed that furniture workers received decent wages and relatively fair treatment. The Greensboro *Labor News* listed a number of High Point furniture factories in its 1909 "Annual Review of the Friendly List," which praised companies that had displayed "a most fair and considerate attitude toward the man who toils."[75]

This more benevolent relationship between management and labor has been accounted for in numerous ways. A writer for the *State* magazine in 1945 argued that it was due to the Quaker background of furniture leaders like that of Tomlinson of High Point who "respected their "employees as persons" and were "concerned about their welfare."[76] Another explanation is that the furniture factories' location within towns and the ability of furniture employees to own their own homes facilitated good relations. Furniture factory workers were not subjected to the deprivations that their counterparts in cotton mill towns of the same period were.

Nevertheless, the furniture industry did not wholly escape labor agitation. Unions found a welcome audience among segments of the poorly paid and vulnerable furniture employees in the state. The Woodworkers Union organized throughout the state along with the Carpenters and Joiners Union.[77] There were also at least two well-documented labor clashes. In 1905, Woodworkers Union members complained about low wages, intermittent work, and the practice of blacklisting by companies. Owners responded by locking out between six hundred and one thousand union members. These union members made appeals to American Federation of Labor leader Samuel Gompers and Governor Robert Brodnax Glenn. But they did not have the organization or resources to stand up to the united furniture manufacturers and they slowly moved to other jobs or abandoned the union.[78] There were also much smaller labor revolts such as a job walkout to protest conditions in Thomasville in 1909.[79] But the labor experience in the North Carolina furniture industry stood in remarkable contrast to that of Grand Rapids, where thousands of workers participated in a massive strike in 1911 that resulted in riots.[80]

A lack of white laborers during the war years forced furniture companies to hire African American men and women. The 1919 *High Point Directory* shows that over thirty African Americans in the city worked as firemen (a job that required tending boilers), watchmen, packers, and fin-ishers.[81] The hiring of African Americans caused consternation in a state dominated by Jim Crow. In 1918, between fifty and sixty white workers walked off the job at the Hickory Chair Company to protest such hiring. The *Hickory Daily Record* noted that the hiring of African Americans was due to "a condition, employers say, that they cannot help."[82]

The next year, union activity led to the most significant labor unrest in High Point history up to that point. Union supporters surrounded the Giant Furniture Company in response to members being locked out of the plant and replaced with scabs.[83] The unrest spread to facto-ries throughout the city. An extra edition of the *High Point Enterprise* asserted that the conflict "practically stopped all payrolls in the city" and that business was at 25 percent of normal.[84] Lockouts only ended when, after the intervention of Governor Walter Bickett, management agreed to a contract with the union. The contract discouraged lockouts and walkouts and granted that "the employees have a right to join any labor union they see fit." It did not, however, demand collective bargaining or allow for the imposition of a closed shop.[85] A writer for the *High Point Enterprise* argued that the picketing was what finally led to the firing of African American men and women from the plants.[86]

By far the most influential development in the furniture industry between 1900 and 1920 was the establishment of the Southern Furni-ture Market in High Point. Such expositions had a long history in the industry, because as William Stevens notes, buyers "liked to see the ac-tual furniture itself, at least at the time of initial selection."[87] Furniture shows began in the 1870s in centers such as Grand Rapids, Michigan, and Jamestown, New York.[88] Once a year, a number of manufacturers would come together and display their pieces in the latest styles. Wholesalers and retailers would make large purchases and commit to further orders over the following months. The expositions helped to set design trends for the next year and facilitated the growth of the industry by connect-ing buyers with sellers. They were also economic engines for the greater region, since some successful furniture expositions attracted furniture professionals from far outside the local area.

The industrial cooperation needed to set up a market saw its begin-

nings in the formation of a group called the Southern Furniture Manufacturers' Association in 1901.[89] This group, dominated by men from
High Point, had trouble organizing and only met once in 1901. But it inspired other cooperative associations including the North Carolina Case
Workers Association (formed in 1905) and another organization called
the Southern Furniture Manufacturers' Association (SFMA), founded in
1911 and not connected to the previous group by the same name. This
industrial cooperation, as William Stevens notes, was a pivotal development in the North Carolina furniture industry's national reputation,
giving the companies that comprised it legitimacy and helping position
them against more established competitors in New York and Grand
Rapids.

The formation of the SFMA brought the furniture industry one of its
longest-serving and most capable leaders. James T. Ryan, a Virginia native, became the organization's executive secretary in 1912 at the age of
twenty-three and went on to lead it for fifty-four years.[90] As its head,
Ryan served as the spokesman for the industry. He was quoted in countless news stories about the performance of the furniture industry and
its role in the state's economy. He traveled to Washington for numerous
lobbying efforts and helped administer industry-related governmental
programs. Ryan also helped individual companies and business leaders
get their start in the industry. He received numerous accolades throughout his career, including a professorship in his name and the de facto
lifetime achievement award from the SFMA, the James T. Ryan Award for
Distinguished Service.

Shortly after its formation, the association won a significant victory
against the nation's railroad companies.[91] Railroads had continuously dis-
criminated against furniture from North Carolina, charging high freight
rates and preventing the state's furniture companies from competing
with their rivals in other regions. The SFMA took the case to the Interstate Commerce Commission and secured a favorable ruling. The *High
Point Enterprise* described the initial Interstate Commerce Commission
meeting as "one of the most important events ever held in the state,"
and Governor Locke Craig mentioned the decision in his 1913 inaugural,
noting that "the city of High Point is to be congratulated that in the ship-

ment of its furniture to the West it will have the same freight rate as rival cities of Virginia."[92]

Partially as a result of the newfound spirit of cooperation and partially as a money-making venture, the first Southern Furniture Market was held in 1909 in downtown High Point.[93] The market was the brainchild of Farriss, Ryan, salesman D. Ralph Parker, and glass manufacturer Charles F. Long.[94] It began in a handful of relatively small spaces including the Millis Building and the Broad Street Furniture Exposition Building.[95] The 1913 Southern Furniture Market counted dozens of furniture companies among its attendees from the nearby states of North Carolina, Virginia, and Georgia and from far away as Connecticut and Oregon.[96] Another one of the city's early furniture shows, billed as the Midsummer Furniture Show, was covered in the *High Point Enterprise* in July 1914. Led by Charles F. Tomlinson, the show operated out of a handful of buildings in downtown High Point and featured displays from over twenty High Point furniture companies and several companies from Lexington, Thomasville, and Greensboro.[97]

After a decade, space demands led the furniture manufacturers of High Point to pool together resources and construct the Southern Furniture Exposition Building on South Main Street. Completed in 1921, the building was one of the most impressive in all of North Carolina. It contained six acres of floor space and housed over a thousand registered buyers by 1925.[98] Designed by Goldsboro architect William P. Rose, the relatively plain building was approximately 170 feet tall with sixteen and a half stories and cost $1 million to build.[99]

By 1921, the furniture industry was a well-established part of North Carolina's industrial economy. The state's 107 furniture factories were being joined by companies and company divisions specializing in marketing, design, and business management.[100] High Point and the rest of the state were gaining an international reputation. But the next three decades would see that reputation, and the overall vitality of the industry, challenged by forces from as far away as Washington and as close as North Carolina's northern neighbor.

FIG. 1. Side chair attributed to Thomas White, early North Carolina cabinet-maker. Museum of Early Southern Decorative Arts Collection, acc. 3381. Gift of Frank L. Horton.

FIG. 2. Desk and bookcase attributed to Lawrence Sarson, an early cabinetmaker working in eastern North Carolina. According to the Museum of Early Southern Decorative Arts, this is the earliest known southern combined desk and bookcase. Museum of Early Southern Decorative Arts Collection, acc. 2377. Anonymous gift.

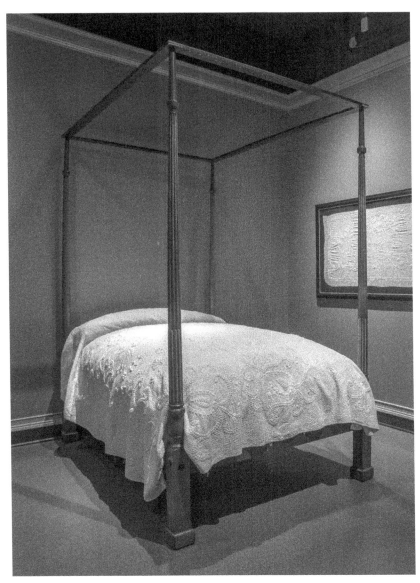

FIG. 3. Bedstead attributed to Richard Hall, a cabinetmaker operating in Halifax. It is a surviving example of work from the Roanoke River Basin School. Museum of Early Southern Decorative Arts collection, acc. 3381. Museum of Early Southern Decorative Arts Purchase Fund.

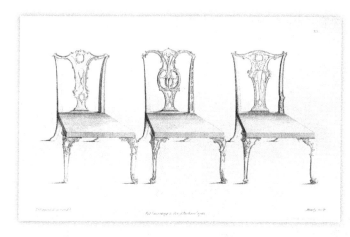

FIG. 4. Side chairs from Thomas Chippendale's guidebook, *The Gentleman and Cabinet-Makers Director* (1754).

FIG.5. Sideboard attributed to Thomas Day, notable for the large S scroll, circa 1840–55. Courtesy of the North Carolina Museum of History.

FIG. 6. Detail from Thomas Day sideboard, circa 1840–55. Courtesy of the North Carolina Museum of History.

FIG. 7. Union Tavern in Milton, built in the early nineteenth century, which served as Thomas Day's workshop for several decades. Author's collection.

FIG. 8. White Furniture Company factory in Mebane. This complex, devastated by fire in 1923, was quickly rebuilt. The factory building is now an apartment complex. Author's collection.

FIG. 9. Continental Furniture Company, one of the earliest High Point furniture factories. Internet Archive.

FIG. 10. Thomas F. Wrenn, one of the founders of the North Carolina furniture industry. Courtesy of American Home Furnishings Hall of Fame Foundation, Inc.

FIG. 11. Alma Desk catalog, circa 1941. Author's collection.

FIG. 12. J. Elwood Cox, early
furniture magnate and 1908
Republican candidate for governor of North Carolina. Internet
Archive.

FIG. 13. Thomas Finch Jr., a
founder of the furniture industry
in Thomasville. Courtesy of the
American Home Furnishings Hall
of Fame Foundation, Inc.

FIG. 14. Chair attributed to the Thomasville Chair Company, late nineteenth century. Courtesy of the North Carolina Museum of History.

FIG. 15. The former Tomlinson Chair Manufacturing Company in High Point, the earliest sections of which were built in the early twentieth century. It now houses Market Square, a furniture showroom complex. Author's collection.

FIG. 16. The former factory of Kemp Furniture in Goldsboro, successor to Goldsboro Manufacturing Company, one of the oldest furniture factories in North Carolina. Author's collection.

FIG. 17. Furniture worker houses in High Point, photographed by Lewis Hine. National Archives.

FIG. 18. Tomlinson of High Point employee running a mechanized sander, photographed by Lewis Hine. National Archives.

FIG. 19. The historic facade of the Southern Furniture Exposition Building, now part of the International Home Furnishings Center, in High Point. Author's collection.

FIG. 20. The big chair in Thomasville, 1951. This steel structure replaced an original wooden chair that was completed in 1922. Author's collection.

FIG. 21. The world's largest chest of drawers in High Point, built in 1926 and remodeled in 1996. The socks were added during remodeling. Author's collection.

FIG. 22. High-quality side table produced by White Furniture, 1938. Courtesy of the North Carolina Museum of History.

FIG. 23. Myrtle Hayworth Barth-maier, one of the first women to lead a furniture company in North Carolina. Courtesy of the American Home Furnishings Hall of Fame Foundation, Inc.

FIG. 24. Child's desk with Formica-top table. Courtesy of the North Carolina Museum of History.

FIG. 25. Modern Danish chairs, reflecting the Scandinavian design philosophy that became influential in North Carolina furniture in the mid-twentieth century. Photo by Linda Glazier, https://www.flickr.com/photos/67302687@N05/6132514233.

FIG. 26. The former headquarters of Broyhill Furniture in Lenoir. This modernist structure was completed in 1966 and vacated by Broyhill in 2011. Author's collection.

FIG. 27. David H. Wagner, the first African American owner of a North Carolina furniture factory, with Dean Blake Morant of Wake Forest University School of Law, circa 2008. Courtesy of Wake Forest University School of Law.

FIG. 28. Bernice Bienenstock Furniture Library in downtown
High Point, opened in 1970. It was originally the Grayson House,
constructed between 1923 and 1925. Author's collection.

FIG. 29. Senator James
Broyhill walking and
talking with President
Ronald Reagan. Wash-
ington, D.C., 1987. Li-
brary of Congress

FIG. 30. Drexel mahogany server produced in Morganton, 1996. Author's collection.

FIG. 31. Former site of Drexel plant no. 1 in Thomasville. Drexel's oldest factory closed in 2001. The site is slated for redevelopment. Author's collection.

FIG. 32. Century Furniture Plant in Hickory. Author's collection.

FIG. 33. The floor of the Tomlinson Erwin-Lambeth furniture factory in Thomasville. Author's collection.

FIG. 34. World's largest highboy dresser, built in 1998 and located at Furnitureland South, Jamestown. Author's collection.

FIG. 35. Wingding, one of the newest designs by Thomasville-based furniture designer David Williams. Courtesy of Trinity Furniture/David Williams.

CHAPTER FOUR ▲▼

The Furniture Market and
the Golden Age, 1920–50

The 1920s was in many ways the golden age of the North Carolina furniture industry. The industry was growing beyond all previous bounds and
was expanding around the world. High Point led the way as always, with
several older towns and a few new centers growing alongside it. Over
the next three decades, through numerous ups and downs, the industry
reached its zenith in the state's economic life. But by the end of that period, the beginning of its decline was already apparent.

High Point during the 1920s exceeded the level of booming success
that it had first garnered in the 1890s. It had twenty-six furniture factories as of 1930.[1] Older concerns such as Tomlinson Chair Manufacturing
Company (which was renamed Tomlinson of High Point in the 1930s) and
the Globe-Home Furniture Company were joined by newer ventures such
as E. W. Lyons Furniture Manufacturing and Rickel Furniture Manufacturing.[2] According to a 1938 report, High Point had the second largest
factory in the state (Tomlinson of High Point) and twelve of the state's
sixty-four factories that employed over one hundred people.[3] The city's
factories worked alongside dealers, repairers, banks, insurance companies, and agents to satisfy nearly every possible demand from the wider
furniture industry.[4]

In High Point, furniture, as well as the city's successful hosiery industry, fueled a number of new companies. Most notable among these was
the Sheraton Hotel, a hotel unrelated to the larger Boston-based chain
and named for the eighteenth-century furniture designer.[5] The Sheraton's purpose was mainly to accommodate visitors attending the furniture exhibition. Its chairs and beds were manufactured in High Point.[6]
The hotel's opening was a significant occasion in the city that attracted
Governor Cameron Morrison as its key speaker.[7] While the hotel was

51

converted into apartments in 1982 and is now a senior living facility, it retains its brick details and neoclassical ornamentation. Over one hundred years after its completion, the structure now known as Sheraton Towers remains one of the twenty tallest buildings in High Point. The Sheraton was joined on the High Point skyline by the Commercial National Bank Building in 1924, a nine-story steel-frame skyscraper with neoclassical details such as long pilasters and an entablature with stone decorations at the top. It housed Commercial National Bank, a furniture-adjacent business owned by J. Elwood Cox, and served as the home of local radio station WMFR beginning in the 1940s.[8]

The Southern Furniture Market, fully established by 1921, drove the town's growth. The market ballooned in size over the next decade or so, owing to both the growing prominence of southern companies and the fact that travel to High Point became easier in this period. By 1936, there were 150 exhibits and over two thousand buyers at the biannual market.[9] Companies attended in 1929 from as far away as New York, Indiana, Ohio, and Michigan.[10] Over thirty types of products were represented, from porch and living room furniture to breakfast room furniture, mirrors, and phonographs.[11] By the 1920s High Point's market was almost as significant as the nation's largest furniture markets in Chicago, New York, and Grand Rapids.[12]

Like many other successful industrial towns, High Point decided to build a monument to the product that had brought it so much fame and prosperity. The town's leaders were inspired by the growing car culture and the related trend of roadside attractions. In 1925, the local chamber of commerce built what was known as the "Bureau of Information," a thirty-six-foot-tall chest of drawers topped with a mirror.[13] The bureau contained a chamber office and remains the world's largest chest of drawers. It retained its initial appearance until 1996, when it was renovated and a pair of giant socks was added to the front in recognition of the city's hosiery industry.

Joining High Point at the vanguard of the state's furniture industry was Thomasville. By 1928, the town had two banks, two business colleges, thirty retailers, and more than thirty insurance agents.[14] The year

1922 saw the construction of the four-story National Bank Building, a sizable neoclassical structure with two large Doric columns.[15] Thomasville was more dominated by the furniture industry than High Point. In 1938, one factory, the Thomasville Chair Company, may have employed more people than the town's entire hosiery and textile companies combined.[16] As in High Point and later Lenoir, the wealth generated by the furniture industry also led to political power. Several members of the Lambeth family, which owned Erwin-Lambeth, entered government, with John Walter Lambeth Jr. representing the area in the U.S. Congress from 1931 to 1939.[17]

As in High Point, Thomasville's leaders decided to build a monument to their most important product. In 1922, the owners of Thomasville's two largest chair companies contributed around $260 to build a giant chair in the town common where it could be seen by both cars on Main Street and passengers traveling on the railroad through town.[18] The chair was first put on display at the 1922 North Carolina State Fair, where it was heavily damaged by students from North Carolina State College (now North Carolina State University). Following the vandalism, the chair was shipped back to Thomasville and repaired.[19] Made of wood, the giant chair rotted over the next twenty years. It was replaced in 1950 by a new chair, made of cement and steel, which survives to this day.[20]

Other towns in the furniture belt also found success. Of the fourteen major towns in it, the average population growth rate during the 1920s was 67 percent.[21] One notable town that grew by more than the average over that decade was Lenoir, the seat of Caldwell County. Lenoir had been a furniture site since 1889, when J. M. Bernhardt and others founded the Lenoir Furniture Company.[22] After floundering in the early twentieth century, Lenoir began to prosper.[23] By 1930, it was the twenty-eighth-largest town in the state and had surpassed other leading furniture-producing towns such as Asheboro and Morganton.[24] Lenoir that year had three banks, six furniture manufacturers, three furniture dealers, and dozens of other businesses.[25]

Much of Lenoir's success can be attributed to James Edgar "Ed" Broyhill, founder of Broyhill Furniture and future leader of the industry. Born in 1892 in Wilkes County, Broyhill lived on the family farm and worked in the lumber business sporadically before serving in the First World War. He received training as a typist in the army and several years of education at the Appalachian Training School (later to become Appalachian State University). He then entered employment at his brother Tom's furniture business in Lenoir in 1919, where for several years he worked as a salesman and bookkeeper.[26]

Seven years later, he started the Lenoir Chair Company.[27] This company had humble beginnings. It was located in a two-story buggy shop. Chair frames were brought in and sprayed on the top floor before being upholstered on the bottom floor.[28] Broyhill then purchased woodworking equipment so he could produce his chairs from lumber. His company soon grew by leaps and bounds, and ten years later, Broyhill took over his brother's company.[29]

Broyhill's firm survived the Great Depression, and after it was over, he started buying up older, bankrupt properties. He purchased the McDowell Furniture Company and the Conover Furniture Company, two of the state's foundational factories, in 1941.[30] A year later, Broyhill bought the building that had housed High Point's first furniture company, which had languished after the death of Manleff J. Wrenn and had recently declared bankruptcy.[31] This purchase symbolized Broyhill's growing success and the beginning of a shift westward in the leadership of the North Carolina furniture industry.

The success of North Carolina firms garnered the attention of their neighbors. During this period, the Virginia and Tennessee furniture industries rose to challenge North Carolina's dominance. Virginia in particular was a formidable foe. Southwest Virginia had many of the same attractive qualities as the western North Carolina Piedmont: abundant lumber, railroads, nearby textile companies, and cheap labor. Its leading company was Bassett Furniture, founded in 1902 by John D. Bassett in a rural area of Henry County. Bassett started producing cheap bedroom furniture in droves.[32] The first plant was soon joined by similar outfits in Martinsville, Altavista, Fieldale, and Galax.[33]

Virginia's furniture industry became the eighth largest in the country for wooden furniture in 1927, only slightly trailing North Carolina at fifth. Virginia's household furniture production increased by more than 28 percent between 1925 and 1927, which exceeded all other states.[34] Virginia joined North Carolina in the 1930s in the turn towards finer furniture. In some ways, the Old Dominion's companies even began to outperform their competitors to the south. In his study of the furniture industry, John James Cater argues that these companies succeeded because they followed and perfected the earlier North Carolina model. The "second wave" of leading furniture companies, which included many from Virginia, he notes, "learned lessons from the first, acquiring knowledge of production methods and marketing skills," and "greatly benefited from the cooperative behavior of potential competitors in an intensely competitive situation."[35] The close familial connections between the Virginia companies largely accounted for this cooperation; almost all of them were located in one or two counties near the North Carolina border and had ties to the Bassett family.

Bassett Furniture was different in several other regards from its neighbors to the south. One was the status of Bassett, Virginia, as a company town. Bassett was unincorporated with no town council to counteract the power of the Bassett family. As Beth Macy argues in her history of Bassett Furniture, "the Bassett rule was arbitrary, completely at the whim of whichever Bassett was calling the shots."[36] By the 1960s, *Fortune* was reporting that Bassett was "one of the last examples of a dying appendage of industry—the company town dominated by a single family. Employees of Bassett Furniture Industries enter the world in a Bassett-endowed hospital, are educated in the John D. Bassett school, live in Bassett houses, work in one of the six local Bassett plants, deposit their savings in a Bassett bank, and worship at the Pocahontas Bassett Baptist Church."[37] None of the major North Carolina furniture towns were company towns like Bassett, and none had the long-term unincorporated status that allowed companies to control every aspect of a town.

Another major difference between Bassett Furniture and North Carolina plants was its scale and approach to manufacturing. The furniture industry in North Carolina was unique among major industries in this time for its reluctance to fully abandon the handicraft model. Production techniques remained stable even as companies began using new technologies and models of industrial organization. The reluctance to embrace vertical integration and combination made economic sense but was also the result of a traditional mindset. Bassett Furniture, on the other hand, embraced new manufacturing developments, attempted to organize its business along modern lines, and represented a larger percentage of the Virginia furniture industry than did any single North Carolina plant. "At the time that Henry Ford established the Ford Motor Company in 1903 for the mass production of automobiles," J. L. Oliver notes, "the brothers Bassett resolved to do likewise in the manufacture of furniture."[38]

The growth of competition from Virginia was felt by North Carolina's furniture companies. The new competitors were making sales in their towns and holding successful exhibitions at their markets. By 1921, a newspaper in Lexington had already identified Bassett Furniture as "one of the largest and most successful furniture manufacturing concerns in the south."[39] But this competition did not stall business for North Carolina companies. Virginia's companies never matched the scale of the companies in North Carolina. According to the 1929 census of manufactures, Virginia had only 54 furniture manufacturing establishments compared with North Carolina's 146.[40] The Old Dominion's industry was concentrated in small towns that did not have the capital and room for expansion that sizable cities like High Point and Hickory did.[41]

Also, the two states' successes were not mutually exclusive. There were more than enough mill villages in the South to serve as markets for furniture produced in two states. Virginia, along with Tennessee, which had its own growing furniture industry, could focus on western markets that did not make financial sense for North Carolina to compete in. The best years for Virginia furniture companies coincided with the best years for companies in High Point and Thomasville.[42]

North Carolina furniture companies in the 1920s and 1930s underwent numerous structural changes that transformed their role in the national industry. One of these was the growth of mechanization, in which had an effect on labor needs. Furniture factories embraced the revolution in electric power that defined American industry in the early twentieth century. In the 1920s, Duke Power built a number of dams on the Catawba River in close proximity to many of the furniture belt's largest towns.[43] The number of electric motors and purchased energy used in the national furniture industry skyrocketed from 7,095 in 1914 to 60,652 in 1929, an increase of over 850 percent.[44]

This new energy source replaced steam power at furniture plants and led to a readier willingness to introduce machines at all stages of the furniture production process. Electric motors eliminated much of the uncertainty and latency surrounding steam engines. Steam engines were belt driven, and the belts could wear down and snap, forcing machines offline. The system for fueling and running steam engines was also complex. Companies had to keep track of the amount of wood refuse available at all times and purchase coal when they found they were running low. Electric motors were not subject to these exigencies and allowed plants to place their machines where they would be most useful and to organize their workflow more efficiently. While companies did not get rid of their boilers and indeed rely on them to this day for recycling wood waste and generating heat for the plant, as Oliver points out, the electric motor meant that "furniture making was liberated from the shaft and belt."[45]

An exhaustive 1948 study of different jobs in the average furniture factory illustrated the trend of mechanization. In the early twentieth century, the vast majority of tasks were still performed by hand. When factories did use machines, they were mainly powered saws, lathes, and other woodworking equipment. A majority of factories did not even have dry kilns throughout the first decades of the twentieth century. By 1948, the standard North Carolina furniture factory had up to fifty different machines in nearly every department. These included sanders, planers, dowel machines, saws, hot-plate veneer presses, glue jointers, conveyers, chair post machines, and dado machines (which cut three-sided grooves into wood for interlocking joints).[46] Mechanization led to larger plants and a slight decrease in reliance on unskilled labor.

Another significant change in the state's industry pertained to design.

By the 1920s, the region was vastly expanded its production of fine furniture. Furniture executive A. P. Haake, in a 1931 article for *Furniture South*, remarked that over the past few years there had been an "increased interest in the decorative improvement in the furniture designs being produced today."[47] Other furniture manufacturers noted a growing interest in colors, detailed veneers, and modern furniture designs, which according to a 1929 *Furniture South* article were becoming so popular that "their modernism no longer attracts attention."[48]

This trend only accelerated in the 1930s when companies started producing historically influenced furniture suites, a trend that owed to the effect of the rebuilding of historic Williamsburg beginning in the 1920s on popular culture. Drexel Furniture Company brought in two designers from Grand Rapids to develop historical styles. They produced pieces inspired by famed English cabinetmakers such as Chippendale, Sheraton, and Hepplewhite as well as by the French designs associated with the reigns of Louis XV and XVI. One of the company's most popular suites in its entire history, the Touraine, was made in the eighteenth-century Louis XV style.[49] These pieces helped Drexel develop a reputation for high-quality pieces that continues to the present day.

Tomlinson of High Point was another pioneer in this field, having introduced a line inspired by colonial Williamsburg in the 1930s.[50] A 1942 catalog, over 180 pages long, details Tomlinson's approach at this time. The catalog is full of all kinds of furniture: beds, chairs, sofas, tables, and desks that could be embellished with wood finishes or upholstery. Many of the Williamsburg-inspired pieces are based on famous historical designs, such as a chair inspired by the George Braxton chair once seen in the Governor's Palace.[51] The catalog also includes neoclassical pieces in a line known as the Kensington Shop. Many of the pieces in this line are advertised as being "authentic interpretations of museum models and original imported antiques in our possession," "made in native fruit and nut woods," and "hand finished in the mellow colors of the period."[52]

Over time, the state's furniture factories came to shape furniture design for a significant portion of the country. Companies introduced their designs at the furniture markets; then retailers purchased what was available and sold those designs in their stores. The millions of dollars brought into High Point through this process fueled other furniture markets in the region, and the Southern Furniture Market remained a resilient source of revenue even when manufacturing faltered.

Economic disincentives to producing cheap furniture in North Carolina also contributed to the shift toward the making of finer pieces. The state's cost benefits were beginning to subside. Material costs increased during the 1920s, mainly due to deforestation and a lack of hardwoods. The state's government agencies and furniture companies became concerned about the declining availability of North Carolina lumber. According to a 1926 report by forest scientist Clarence F. Korstian, the amount of imported wood used in the state's furniture industry increased from 5 percent in 1909 to 31 percent in 1919: "There is less suitable furniture timber in this State now than there was ten years ago; prices are from 100 to 200 percent higher; cheaper woods are being substituted for the more expensive, and in some cases metal is being substituted for wood; and the manufacturers are looking to more distant forests for their supply of raw material."[53]

These changes, according to Korstian, would lead to a reckoning in the state's furniture industry. With much of the cheaper hardwoods requiring shipment from the Mississippi Valley and further west, Korstian predicted that the industry would start building finer furniture from locally produced, more expensive woods such as black walnut, improve its production methods, and start buying timber from government-sanctioned tree farms: "The tendency is toward a fairly rapid change to a production of more of the better grades of furniture. This is stimulated by the fact that raw materials are now but little cheaper in the Piedmont region than elsewhere, and by the fact that now skilled operatives can not profitably be kept at work on a cheap product at the high wages prevailing at present."[54]

After fluctuations in the 1920s, wages steadily grew in the late 1930s and jumped by 150 percent in the 1940s.[55] Higher wages created more incentives to bring in machinery, train workers, and build higher-quality pieces with larger profit margins. It is true, as John G. Selby points out, that furniture wages in North Carolina were 75 percent of the national average.[56] Furniture employees were not wealthy by any means, and some remained poor. But still, on average, they were paid eleven cents more per hour than textile workers.[57]

The textile industry mainly produced coarse products such as denims and towels that had low profit margins. Consequently, price was the primary means of competition. As Brent Glass argues, textile producers in the state "were more interested in reducing their cost per unit than in controlling the quantity of their output."[58] The furniture industry, on the other hand, could compete on price as well as design and quality. It was shipping products far outside of the low-wage and low-price markets that had originally sustained it in North Carolina; Tomlinson of High Point, for instance, shipped 97 percent of its products out of the state in 1944.[59] The industry therefore had the latitude to pay higher wages and use more skilled workers than the textile industry. The furniture industry had developed significantly since its low-quality roots in the late nineteenth century, and its new scope would determine its approach to business and labor in the 1930s and beyond.

The furniture industry certainly treated white workers better than the textile industry did in the early twentieth century. But for African Americans, the record was more mixed. There was a purge of war-era African American workers soon after 1918, but in the subsequent decade furniture factories began to hire increasing numbers of Black workers as the demand for labor grew. City directories from the 1920s show a considerable number of African American employees at furniture companies. The 1930 *High Point City Directory* lists more than seventy-five African American furniture workers and drivers. Many of these men and women worked at several of the city's largest and most notable factories, from the Globe-Home Furniture plant to the High Point Furniture Company and the Knox Furniture Company.[60] As in earlier years, rates of African American work in the industry were similar in every town except Winston-Salem, where they were higher because of the larger Black population in that city. A 1949 article in the *Carolinian* also noted that there were two African American buyers at that year's Southern Furniture Market.[61]

While African Americans gained access into the ranks of furniture workers, they were excluded from the privileged group of factory owners. In textiles, Warren Clay Coleman started one of the first plants owned and staffed by African Americans in 1898.[62] Coleman's plant was joined by the Durham Textile Mill (1904) and a handful of hosiery mills.[63] There were no such early pioneers for the furniture industry. In fact, perhaps the only pre-1945 furniture factory in the nation owned by African Americans was located in Los Angeles.[64] In the Jim Crow South, prospective African American factory owners ran up against the same barriers that other Black businessmen faced. Furniture factories required business connections and a considerable amount of hard-to-obtain starting capital, unlike the insurance companies and service industries that built much of the wealth for the region's Black Wall Streets.[65]

One unique entrant into the field of factory ownership was Myrtle Hayworth Barthmaier, one of the first women to run a North Carolina furniture factory.[66] She took over the Alma Desk Company following the death of her husband in 1928 and led it for several decades. Myrtle made several business deals and was seen as a success in the position.[67] An even more successful female furniture executive was Katherine Lambeth. She became the first president of the consolidated Erwin-Lambeth company in 1947. Under her leadership, Erwin-Lambeth produced some of the highest-quality furniture pieces of any Thomasville company.[68]

The Great Depression devastated the North Carolina furniture industry like all other sectors of the American economy. Fears of an economic slowdown were evident prior to the stock market crash. *Furniture South* noted a weak market in January 1929.[69] Later that year, Grand Rapids furniture leader C. B. Hamilton observed that there was a "sickness" in the business, one that had many potential sources and just as many possible remedies, including "decreased stocks allowing the manufacturer to carry the burden—the easing of overhead in the discharging of clerks and the lessening of rent—better cost finding methods—better educated salesmen."[70] Even with many of those solutions in place, Hamilton noted a fear among many executives that "the patient is still sick."[71] These fears were well founded, for in the first three years of the Depression 50 percent of furniture workers were either laid off or fired.[72]

The financial records of Tomlinson Chair Manufacturing Company illustrate the impact of the Depression on the furniture business. Tomlinson was one of the largest and most successful furniture companies of the twentieth century. In 1928, it recorded sales of over $2 million and a profit of over $50,000.[73] Four years later, another audit showed the ravages of the Depression on furniture fortunes. Sales had plummeted to under $400,000 for the first six months of 1932. The factory was now losing on average $150,000 every six months, and it had significantly cut its sales force and administrative expenses as well.[74] The note along with the auditor's report pointed out that further "reductions in number of employees and in wage rates . . . have already been put into effect."[75]

Closures and wage cuts also broke the uneasy peace between capital and labor in the furniture industry. The most strikes in the industry's history took place in 1932. Workers went on strike in High Point and at the massive Thomasville Chair Company.[76] But because the relationship between capital and labor had been good up to this point, the size of these actions was smaller than in the textile industry, which saw thousands of workers picketing in 1934.[77] The Thomasville workers refused to cooperate with striking cotton mill workers.[78] There was no bloodshed—in contrast, seven people died in the textile strikes of 1929—and most of the company's workers went back to the factory after three weeks.[79] The High Point furniture strike ended relatively quickly due to the financial stability of the workers. As historian John G. Selby observes, furniture workers did not see the strike as "their fight." They were happy that "they finally had some steady hours as plants prepared for the rush of orders that accompanied the annual furniture market show held in High Point in July."[80]

Franklin Roosevelt's New Deal, while opposed by the conservative furniture industry, ended up revitalizing it by the mid-1930s. New Deal reforms such as the National Industrial Recovery Act and the Works Progress Administration increased consumer demand, raised prices, decreased the massive surplus of furniture languishing in warehouses, and stemmed the bankruptcies of furniture companies.[81] The New Deal restarted the discretionary spending that the state's furniture industry relied on.

One Works Progress Administration program in particular irked furniture manufacturers even more than wage and production regulations. Under this program, a set of furniture factories were to be opened and operated by the federal government in places such as Cherry Lake, Florida; Knoxville, Tennessee; and Reedsville, West Virginia.[82] These factories would produce different products but would all have the common goal of supplying relief to the unemployed. Nevertheless, they were seen as undue competition by furniture manufacturers throughout the country, with North Carolinian business owners frequently taking the lead in opposition.

Furniture manufacturers particularly objected to the Reedsville plant for producing post office furniture, a humanitarian project Eleanor Roosevelt undertook to aid unemployed coal miners.[83] Harold Ickes, the U.S. secretary of the interior, surmised that the plant in Reedsville would add 125 jobs.[84] Furniture manufacturers, however, decried the Reedsville plant and the overall plan as "state socialism." It was seen as a violation of the industrial codes that governed the opening and operation of new plants.[85] After lobbying by James T. Ryan, North Carolina senator Josiah Bailey, and North Carolina representative John Walter Lambeth Jr., the House eventually voted against federal funding for the plan.

Advances in labor law also fueled numerous belated union drives in the state. The Wagner Act created protections for workers who wanted to form unions. Furniture labor responded accordingly by establishing a new union, the Congress of Industrial Organizations, which was affiliated with the United Furniture Workers of America.[86] Workers at Tomlinson of High Point in 1946 and Thomasville Chair Company in 1942 attempted to set up union elections via the National Labor Relations Board with both the United Furniture Workers of America and its American Federation of Labor counterparts.[87] The record was mixed: Thomasville's workers voted in favor of the union and Tomlinson's against it; in both instances, workers were influenced by a dogged campaign from management.[88] These elections, like the *Bailey v. Drexel Furniture Company* case in 1922, showed the obstinance and conservatism of the furniture companies, which were inclined to treat their workers decently but vigorously resisted any attempt by outside forces to compel even better treatment.

By the late 1930s, the industry was on the rebound. Many of the supporting businesses were much healthier as a result of the New Deal. Bank closures across the nation dropped substantially, from a high of 2,737 in 1933 down to just 34 in 1935.[89] Transportation, machine manufacturing, and heavy industry all started to bounce back. These more successful industries helped provide the infrastructure and to create the demand that made it possible for furniture companies to thrive once again. A 1935 analysis reported that by that year, the industry had begun its recovery and had "freed itself almost entirely from bankruptcy losses."[90] Between 1937 and 1939, employment in the industry improved by about 10 percent.[91] The Southern Furniture Exposition Center reported successful markets in 1934 and 1935.[92] Other furniture markets around the country also showed significant gains over the next few years.[93]

The southern furniture industry recovered more quickly from the Depression than the northern. While southern manufacturers had started to embrace finer products by the 1930s, the vast majority of output from southern factories was still cheap and utilitarian. There was a demand for these pieces, since new homes were still being built and old furniture still needed to be replaced. But as during the 1857 panic, demand for luxury goods dropped precipitously, and companies in Grand Rapids and Chicago made more of their profits from these higher-priced goods than did southern companies. Stevens notes that the attachment to quality led Grand Rapids to eschew many of the time- and labor-saving developments that the South was beginning to embrace by the 1930s and 1940s. Northern and midwestern furniture factories could not compete on price or meet the demand of the lower-quality markets as the southern companies could.

The Second World War threatened to erase much of this recovery. Following the declaration of war in December 1941, the nation's economy turned to preparation and mobilization. Companies were forbidden from using metal and other materials needed for the war effort. Luxuries such as ornate cabinets and chests of drawers were frowned on.[94] The industry was forced to adapt. As early as 1942, furniture companies started to transition to building parts for the war effort. A March 1942 article in the *High Point Enterprise* noted that "virtually all furniture manufacturers have been looking towards conversion to some vital defense industry," such as airplane and boat parts made of wood.[95]

In this trying time, the Southern Furniture Manufacturers' Association turned to Ed Broyhill just as it had to Charles F. Tomlinson during the First World War.[96] Broyhill had been cultivating political contacts throughout the Depression, and he put them to use after 1941. The Lenoir businessman secured agreements from the War Production Board that allowed furniture companies to obtain supplies and remain in business.[97] He also made the case in 1945 that the industry should be permitted to increase prices; the federal government was persuaded, and many companies therefore avoided bankruptcy. With Broyhill's aid, dozens of companies found a way to work with the federal government to provide products for the war effort. In 1943, the leaders of Drexel Furniture Company noted that 60 percent of their output consisted in products for the war. These products included airplane parts as well as "locks, gunstocks, truck bodies, life rafts, ammunition boxes, bomb boxes, tent pins, rolling pins, and furniture items, especially office desks and chairs."[98]

A 1942 book, *Woodworking for War*, advertises the materials and labor resources present in High Point to aid the war effort. Its sponsor, the High Point Furniture and Woodworking Association, commissioned the book because despite their patriotism, "wood fabricators have faced perplexing problems in enlisting their resources most effectively. What are the specific products and quantities required? By what procedure can the proper source of supply be joined to the national need? . . . [R]ather than wait inactively, members of this Association already have grouped their plants and facilities for such enlistment as will best advance the nation's war activities."[99] The book begins by giving an overview of High Point, its residents, power facilities, and industries, noting that High Point was at the center of hardwood production and had all of the modern amenities a town devoted to war production would need, such as sophisticated infrastructure and transportation facilities.[100] High Point's residents were also perfect for the task at hand: "There are countless employees whose forbears were identified with the industry 55 years ago. Familiarity with the tools of woodworking, the materials, and later the machinery, are virtually a heritage of literally thousands of factory employees."[101] The book goes on to document the thirty-three different types of woodworking equipment in the town, as well as the size, capabilities, and labor makeup of thirty-four different furniture and furniture-related companies. It is no wonder that after this pitch, the War Production Board accepted High Point's offer and requisitioned war materials from the town.[102]

In 1948, the Southern Furniture Market returned to normal operations after a relaxation of wartime quotas and buying restrictions. The state's furniture factories were unprepared for what would come next. The 1950s proved to be one of the most profitable and forward-thinking decades in the industry's history. But the industry's flaws, some of which had been evident since the 1920s, started to become more troubling for the companies that meant so much to the economic health and social system of North Carolina's furniture belt.

CHAPTER FIVE

Pressure and Competition, 1950–80

In 1960, presidential candidate John F. Kennedy became one of the most famous people ever to visit the furniture region of North Carolina. He and his running mate Lyndon Johnson visited several furniture towns in the then-battleground state. Kennedy's visit was brief: he touched down at the airport in western Greensboro, greeted thousands of supporters, and then flew to Asheville.[1] Lyndon Johnson took a whistle-stop tour of the furniture region, stopping in High Point, Thomasville, and Lexington.[2] In High Point, Johnson gave a brief speech and greeted hundreds of visitors along with Governor Luther Hodges and future governor Terry Sanford. Johnson attracted an even larger crowd at Thomasville, where he climbed into that town's big chair with a ladder provided by the fire department.[3]

This candidate visit showcased the power and influence the North Carolina furniture industry had gained by 1960. It had long since become North Carolina's third largest industry, and the state was in the process of becoming the nation's furniture capital. But general prosperity for the state's furniture factories did not mean equal prosperity for all companies, regions, and workers. A number of trends began in the 1950s and 1960s that, by the late 1970s, placed the industry in an unstable position.

The prosperity of the 1950s allowed the furniture industry to thrive. The GI Bill, transportation changes, the baby boom, and pent-up demand from the war years led to an explosion in housing construction.[4] All of these houses needed furniture. Economic prosperity meant that Americans had more money with which to buy furniture of all types and prices. Americans were spending more time at home, which meant a greater demand for objects used within the home. The growing trends of planned obsolescence and conspicuous consumption, fueled by a boom in advertising, pushed Americans to buy more furniture in the latest styles. The average years of usage for furniture dropped.

North Carolina furniture companies responded accordingly to this new demand. Companies ramped up production and expanded the types of pieces they were crafting. There was new furniture in modern styles as well as the early American, which had remained popular ever since the rebuilding of Williamsburg. By 1967, one-third of all furniture bought in the United States was in the early American style.[5] Companies like Magnavox and Tomlinson were manufacturing newer products like television cabinets and stereo furniture.[6]

Companies were beginning to embrace a wide variety of modern design styles. One of these was the Scandinavian model, mainly attributed to Danish furniture designers. Leading Danes in the furniture industry such as Rudolf Rasmussen and Kaare Klint imported sparse modern designs with clean lines and adopted a comprehensive approach to interior space. Other Danish designers such as Eero Saarinen introduced bold, organic curvilinear forms using new materials for furniture.[7] It was the Scandinavian influence that helped modern furniture styles gain greater acceptance and shed their earlier niche status. Scandinavian-inspired designs were taken up by a variety of furniture manufacturers such as Broyhill, Drexel, and Henredon. There were also Scandinavian companies, although the most famous of these companies today, Ikea, did not open an American location until 1985.

North Carolina furniture manufacturers began using the newest synthetic materials in their pieces. These materials were inexpensive, easy to clean, and formed the basis for the most stylish and modern designs in the field. One of the most famous was Formica, a material composed of a paper or textile base mixed with a hard plastic resin.[8] Tables with Formica tops became ubiquitous in the state's furniture industry, and it along with other synthetic materials came to dominate catalogs and product offerings. *Furniture South* reported that from 1955 to 1966, the market for one particular synthetic product (melamine laminates) grew

9 percent per year to a total of $60 million.[9] In 1972, a sample catalog of new furniture in that same magazine contained a wide variety of synthetic materials such as laminated plastic tops, polydacron seating cushions, and polyurethane foam.[10]

A number of companies also began to use particle board. This material was made of wood shavings, chips, and refuse from the manufacturing process combined with a resin. It helped companies create lightweight, inexpensive designs—prices for particle board in the 1970s were on par with those for standard lumber and plywood—while also conserving environmental resources and making use of the factory's waste products. Furniture factory owners were defensive of particle board's quality, which was sometimes derided as weak and flimsy.[11] Regardless of its reputation, particle board became a cheap, ubiquitous material in many products beyond furniture, from flooring to doors, speakers, and guitar cases.

New materials and sources of profit led to a change in the fundamental structure of the North Carolina furniture industry. Several large companies, attracted by the recently enhanced revenue and perceived lack of competition, started to build and sell furniture. One of the most prominent was textile giant Burlington Industries. This company, formed in 1924 by James Spencer Love, entered the furniture industry in 1966 when it purchased the famed Globe-Home Furniture Company in High Point. Burlington bought the even larger United Furniture Company of Lexington in 1968 and National Upholstery of High Point in 1971. With such large furniture businesses complementing its already expansive textile holdings, in 1972 Burlington proclaimed itself the national leader in home furnishings.[12]

Burlington was joined by several other large companies that wanted to consolidate a set of consumer products in one company. Burlington produced textiles and furniture in order to provide all the home furnishings that a family needed. Magnavox, another large entrant into the field, wanted to provide every aspect of the television-watching experience, from the machine itself to the cabinet that housed it. Other large companies that became involved in the furniture industry had a variety of connections, such as to wood processing (Mead) and carpet (Mohasco).[13] By the late 1970s, the large conglomerates had captured a significant percentage of the national furniture market and were threatening North Carolina's industrial structure.

These entrants caused unease in the furniture belt. Near the beginning of the trend in 1969, Reginald Styers warned of the impact that large companies could have on the industry. He noted that the large companies, the "conglomerates and 'super conglomerates,'" were slowly taking over the industry, and although they had promised "that each organization within its combine will still function as usual on its own," nothing was guaranteed. Styers was focused more on the quality of products than the survival of jobs, asking, "will it eventually be that furniture styles and types will have no more distinction than the automobile industry?"[14]

Sharing Styers's skepticism, traditional furniture executives also looked with scorn on many of the new entrants. Furniture executive O. William Fenn Jr. noted that in the early years of conglomerates, "None of those things worked, because, at that point at least, the furniture business was so much of a proprietary kind of business. . . . [T]here was no real manufacturing synergy between the companies because they really were too different."[15] According to Douglas Brackett of the American Furniture Manufacturers Association, new companies like Burlington tried to bring up-to-date scientific management techniques into an industry that had not used them before. The results were problematic. As Brackett notes in a 2009 oral history interview, "I remember a guy from Mead Paper came down after they had bought Stanley [a Virginia furniture company]. He wanted to know how many king-sized beds, queen-sized beds, single beds, trundle beds, bunk beds and chests were made every year. I said, 'I don't have any idea.' He said: 'What? You don't know? I can tell you how many reams of paper were produced by the paper industry last year.' I said, 'I suspect you can because you're all publicly held.' None of our guys to speak of were publicly held. . . . So you wound up with some frustrated people who bought into the industry without doing their homework first, who wanted to know all this detailed marketing information."[16]

Despite their failures, companies like Burlington had the ability to withstand temporary losses in a way that their smaller, local competitors did not. Other smaller companies started to merge and grow larger. They took advantage of their success to branch out into different areas of furniture production. Drexel Furniture Company was a prime example of this trend. In the 1950s, Drexel's profits grew from $18 million per year to $43 million.[17] Drexel acquired Morganton Furniture in 1957 and Southern Desk Company in 1961.[18] By the early 1960s, the company, which had become Drexel Enterprises, also became known for its practice of introducing specific brands and for its advertising of those brands to the public.

It was difficult for many of the older companies to compete with the growing national conglomerates. Consequently, several were sold in the 1960s and 1970s. The most notable of these was Drexel Enterprises, which despite its success and growth was purchased by U.S. Plywood-Champion Papers, a northern wood-product conglomerate, in 1968. That same year, Armstrong Cork, one of the country's largest ceiling, flooring, and insulation companies, purchased Thomasville Furniture Industries (formerly Thomasville Chair Company).[19] These purchases broke the North Carolina–centric mold that had been part of the industry since its founding. But at first, they did not threaten the basis of the industry. Many of the purchased companies including Drexel Enterprises (renamed Drexel Heritage after its acquisition) and Globe-Home Furniture continued to produce large quantities of furniture and employ considerable numbers of local employees.

Companies also began to expand outside of the state's traditional furniture belt. Demand as well as changes in transportation aided this expansion. By the 1970s, the main highways of the furniture belt, most notably US 64 and US 70 but also I-85, had been completed and stretched from Hot Springs and Murphy in the west to Morehead City and Manteo in the east.[20] Better transportation led to more customers and more extensive supply lines that allowed factories to operate far from timber stands. At the same time, local markets grew, supported by general postwar prosperity and the strength of tobacco and cotton mills. These factors led to more furniture production in far-flung areas. By 1968, factories stretched from Bryson City east to Washington. There were over a dozen towns with furniture factories east of Raleigh and more than half a dozen west of the traditional western boundary of the industry at Marion.[21]

Changes in furniture organization, structure, and production were all influenced by new government regulation of the industry. In the 1970s, government agencies began to take a hard look at occupational safety and environmental effects of furniture factories. Regulators imposed emissions standards for wood dust and chemicals such as nitrogen dioxide and sulfur dioxide.[22] They commissioned studies that measured the health effects of woodworking, the use of finishes, and the loud noises made by furniture machines. Companies began a decades-long effort to win favorable regulatory hearings on finishes and worker health in particular.

Leading the way in the new furniture business was Ed Broyhill. The Lenoir-based furniture executive had steadily grown his business throughout the Depression and postwar years. His success only continued to grow during the postwar boom. Broyhill Industries' profits grew from $75 million per year in 1966 to over $265 million per year by the end of the 1970s.[23] His salesmen traveled throughout the country and became a fixture at furniture markets in Chicago and New York. Broyhill was named man of the year in 1946 by the American Furniture Mart board of governors and was profiled in 1957 by the magazine *Wood and Wood Products* as part of its "Wood Salutes" feature.[24]

Broyhill's company patented some of the 1950s' most significant production developments. One was the monorail conveyor belt in the finishing department, which moved pieces between spray stations so coats of varnish could be applied more conveniently.[25] At around the same time, the Broyhill company introduced the hot-plate press, which made plywood construction simpler. Before, veneered furniture had been seen as inferior to solid furniture, since it used only a small amount of high-quality wood and could also easily peel apart. Broyhill's process, according to William Stevens, "overcame virtually all objections to the use of veneers and established a favorable quality comparison between solid and veneered furniture."[26]

Broyhill also cultivated a variety of political connections. He became friends with Senator Kenneth Wherry in the 1940s. This friendship led to relaxed regulations for the furniture industry throughout the war years and generally favorable terms soon after.[27] Broyhill was also a close supporter of Ohio senator Robert Taft. Because of his connections with Taft, Broyhill played golf with President Dwight Eisenhower in 1953 and started a long-lasting correspondence.[28] In 1967, as part of an event honoring Broyhill's decades as a Republican committeeman, Richard Nixon wrote, "the Republican Party is in your debt for the thousands of hours of service you have given us as a national committeeman."[29]

Ed Broyhill's many political connections were put to use by his son, James. After years working at his father's company and supporting several community organizations such as the Jaycees and the Lenoir Chamber of Commerce, "Jim" Broyhill ran for Congress in 1962 and won as a Republican in the Democratic Solid South.[30] He moved up through Republican party politics in the 1960s and 1970s, becoming one of the state's most well-known Republicans.

Ed Broyhill's leadership was a symbol of the general growth of western North Carolina furniture towns; as Stevens observes, in the 1940s, "as the furniture manufacturing industry migrated down the Appalachian range in search of lumber and labor, it met Ed Broyhill coming up the mountain."[31] Lenoir and Hickory followed the trend of hiring cheap labor and reducing costs that had benefited High Point in the 1900s the most closely. Lenoir's population nearly doubled between 1950 and 1970. It had Broyhill as well as Kent-Coffey Manufacturing, Bernhardt Furniture, and the largest furniture factory in the state, a division of the national Magnavox company known as Consolidated Furniture Industries.[32] Instead of having a central market like High Point did, several of the town's leading factories had their own markets where visitors could see the latest lines. Buyers visited the markets in the days before the major Southern Furniture Market in High Point and brought a considerable amount of business to western towns like Lenoir.[33] The town became home to one of the largest furniture buildings in the state outside of High Point, the new Broyhill headquarters and showroom, in 1966.

Hickory grew substantially over the mid-twentieth century as well.

By the 1970 census, the town's population had reached twenty thousand, and it had more than seventy furniture factories as of 1968.[34] Companies in the town such as Century Furniture and Hickory Springs Manufacturing, both founded in the 1940s, went on to become some of the nation's largest.[35] Furniture industry success contributed to a building boom in Hickory, including what is now known as the Wells Fargo Building with its stark Brutalist facade, which was built in 1974. By the 1970s, Hickory was often referred to as the secondary center of the furniture industry behind High Point.[36]

The most visible symbol of Hickory's growth was the establishment of the Hickory Furniture Mart in 1960. This market started out as a gathering place for furniture wholesalers in the basement of Mull's Restaurant but soon became popular enough to warrant the construction of a three-hundred-thousand-square-foot exhibition space.[37] The exhibition space was doubled by a new addition built in 1976.[38] The biannual Hickory Furniture Mart attracted eighty exhibitors by 1975 and was seen as a smaller but strong competitor to the market in High Point.[39] Hickory was popular enough to sustain a second major market, the Hickory Home Furnishings Mart, which began operating in 1963 with space for more than twenty exhibitors.[40]

Smaller western furniture towns such as Morganton and Marion were profitable as well. The advent of interstate highways helped these towns attract employees and customers from a much wider area. In many towns, furniture companies were the primary economic engine. Furniture factories in West Jefferson, Stoneville, and Bryson City employed at least 250 employees, which was more than 20 percent of the entire population of these towns. Ronda's factory in 1970 employed between 250 and 500, a sizable amount for a town of fewer than 500 residents.[41] Even though many employees commuted to these towns, just as many others lived there. These were furniture towns in much the same way as Burlington and Concord were textile towns and Durham and Scotland Neck were tobacco towns.

The growth of Lenoir and other western furniture centers did not lead to a failure of older centers. Instead, the shift was relative. While western towns were growing faster, eastern towns still had a considerable furniture manufacturing sector. High Point still had more than a hundred furniture factories according to a 1968 manufacturer's directory, the most in North Carolina.[42] Thomasville had over twenty factories, and Lexington had more than a dozen.[43]

Some individual companies in the eastern furniture belt also found great success. White Furniture Company remained one of the state's most successful, shipping high-quality pieces around the world and receiving attention in national magazines such as *House Beautiful* and *Better Homes and Gardens*.[44] Globe-Home Furniture opened a massive new building in High Point prior to the 1964 Southern Furniture Market.[45] In nearby Lexington, Dixie Furniture remained one of the state's five largest plants with more than a thousand employees.[46]

High Point continued to embrace the Southern Furniture Market as its claim to fame. The Exposition Building received a massive add-on in 1966 with the completion of the Green Street wing, which brought the total amount of display space in the exhibition center to more than one million square feet.[47] A 1963 list of buyers attending that year's spring market showcased the breadth and scope of furniture attendees. The list included thousands of names from hundreds of different companies; buyers from forty-five states plus the District of Columbia and over one thousand buyers from North Carolina alone attended.[48] States with high attendance numbers included nearby states such as Virginia with more than four hundred buyers, and more distant states such as New York with approximately the same number.[49] Foreign companies were also represented, including from France, Italy, and Canada.[50] Over the next decade, High Point eclipsed Chicago as the largest furniture market in the nation.[51] The international presence at the Southern Furniture Market also continued to grow; by 1975, it was attracting companies from fifteen to twenty countries, and the fall 1975 market opened with an old-fashioned English town crier.[52]

Despite High Point's successes, though, the future of furniture manufacturing was clearly in the west. Thirteen of the eighty largest firms in the state were in Lenoir.[53] Technological innovations came from Broyhill's companies, while many companies in the vanguard of design were in western centers such as Drexel and Hazelwood.[54] With the west taking hold of manufacturing, High Point and older furniture centers also started to move toward marketing, research and development, and design during this period. The number of employees engaged in these areas ballooned in the 1960s. Slightly smaller firms that were concerned with quality, such as Lambeth (Erwin-Lambeth after 1947) in Thomasville and Thayer Coggin in High Point, became immensely profitable.[55] The shift away from large-scale manufacturing and toward higher-quality manufacturing and skilled services was in line with the national economic shift during the 1970s toward a service-based economy.

In an attempt to encourage further marketing and design development as well as to improve management, the furniture industry began to invest in education. At a well-attended ceremony before the 1970 spring Southern Furniture Market, N. I. Bienenstock opened a furniture library in High Point, the largest in the world, to help make available several centuries' worth of knowledge about furniture design.[56] One of the earliest furniture-specific curriculums in the state was a joint four-year degree program offered by North Carolina State College and the University of North Carolina in 1946. This program, designed with the help of the Southern Furniture Manufacturers' Association, focused on management and production techniques.[57] There were two tracks: an industrial engineering degree track for students who stayed at North Carolina State College for their third and fourth years, and a business management track at the University of North Carolina.[58] The university business courses were mostly general, while furniture-specific courses covering such topics as lumber seasoning, gluing and plywood, and wood technology were offered at the college, either in the first two years of the general program or in the last two years of the industrial engineering track.[59]

North Carolina State College became a leading center for furniture studies and research in the postwar decades. By 1950, the joint program with the University of North Carolina had influenced the formation of the Furniture Manufacturing and Management Center in the Department of Industrial Engineering at North Carolina State College, which offered a major of the same name. The center was led for over a decade by Professor E. Sigurd Johnson, a leading woodworking engineer who patented a particle board process.[60] The college's program grew modestly over the next two decades. It went from offering six directly furniture-related courses in 1956 to nine in 1977, while the number of furniture professors rose from one (plus a visiting lecturer) to three.[61] As of 1961, North Carolina State College's was the only furniture training program of its kind in the nation.

The program at North Carolina State College (which became North Carolina State University in 1965) was later joined by similar ones at community colleges across the furniture region. Some of the most notable programs were at Caldwell Technical Institute in Lenoir and Catawba Valley Technical College in Hickory. Catawba Valley became a leading center for furniture design, while Caldwell Technical received special praise from Broyhill Industries for its ability to train new supervisors by offering courses that "range all the way from improvement in basic English . . . to highly specialized technical woodworking."[62] But smaller schools also had impressive furniture course listings, with Randolph Technical Institute in Asheboro offering three courses in furniture design and a furniture-oriented interior design associate's degree by 1977.[63]

The westward shift in the state's furniture industry helps to explain why furniture executives' prediction in the 1920s that wages in the industry would go up did not come true. These executives believed that the finer products demanded by a more affluent consumer base and more sophisticated companies would require experienced craftsmen and that higher labor costs, along with higher material costs, would thus follow. But by 1950, furniture wages were some of the lowest in the state. A 1952 report from the North Carolina Department of Labor noted that the hourly wage for furniture workers was $1.10, ten cents below the state average.[64] Even the textile industry, which was profiled in the *New York Times* as one of the worst-paying industries in the nation, paid more per hour than the furniture industry for several decades.[65] In 1956, 49 percent of all furniture workers made less than $1 an hour, while only 15 percent of textile workers did.[66] By 1972, wages in the furniture industry had surpassed those in the textile industry, but they were still six cents below the average for factory jobs.[67]

The western shift in the furniture industry played an important role in this low-wage regime. It created more basic, low-wage jobs faster than the Piedmont could create higher-quality, more skilled jobs. The low levels of automation in the industry actually hurt wages over time. The furniture industry was loath to use even basic forms of automation like conveyor belts. Some of this reluctance was due to stubbornness and a lack of education in small towns, but most came from the inability to create automated furniture production machines with the same ease as the automobile or textile industries.

Higher quality did not help the situation. Even though many companies made high-quality pieces and the bottom-line pieces from the early twentieth century mostly disappeared, supply was high relative to demand, and using fewer machines led to less need for skilled, highly paid staff. There was a vicious cycle: low wages meant companies had no pressure to automate, meaning that they could continue hiring unskilled employees and pay those employees low wages.[68] In addition to wages being low generally, not surprisingly, there was also a gender pay gap in the furniture industry as in other industries, and so women were paid considerably less than their male counterparts. This discrimination against women was amplified in the subfield of upholstered furniture, where piecework was more common. The practice of paying an incentive to every employee for every chair or cushion they finished led to the occasional high salary. But in general, it produced a rushed atmosphere prone to abuse and injury.[69]

The pervasively small size of furniture factories played a role in the low wages the industry paid as well. Even though towns like Lenoir had large factories, the majority of factories were small outfits in mountain towns. Many factories did not have enough capital to pay for mechanization. Furthermore, the industry's small cadre of workers did not have a tradition of unionizing and therefore did not organize for better treatment or pay.

The industry's need to accommodate a large number of buyers who purchased pieces based on price above everything else at the expositions also promoted a low-wage regime. In his analysis of the furniture industry, Steven S. Plice argues that the enormous amount of competition the biannual markets generated guided the furniture industry's labor policies, resulting in "a management profoundly sensitive to any cost increases, including wages and employee benefits."[70]

The barriers to entry in a labor-intensive industry like furniture were low. Once again, the biannual markets played a role. Companies refused to automate because they had to change their styles too often to ensure they were always presenting something new every six months.[71] Therefore, new companies could easily set up a factory with little capital tied up in machinery, pay their workers minimal wages, and capture a considerable share of market interest. Since these manufacturers appealed to retailers and almost never to the consumer, brand loyalty was not a factor. Shoppers felt loyalty to brands such as Sears Roebuck or Montgomery Ward, companies that bought designs at the market and then put their own brands on the pieces. As a result, even large companies felt the need to compete with the smallest outfits on price, resulting in a persistent cap on wages.

Another factor in low wages was the inability of unions to gain a foothold in the state's furniture industry. North Carolina's industry management had always been hostile to unions, and by the mid-twentieth century the state was known as the least labor-friendly state in the nation. By the 1950s, the Congress of Industrial Organizations had launched Operation Dixie, a plan to unionize workers across the South and on both sides of the color line. The plan was most famously directed at the textile industry, but furniture employees were also courted throughout North Carolina.

There was the occasional union victory, such as the elections at Kay Manufacturing in 1958 and Statesville Plywood and Veneer Company in 1964, both of which resulted in the formation of a union with bargaining power.[72] But for the most part, furniture factories avoided labor strife by implementing the same personally caring yet conservative approach to employee relations that characterized the early decades of the industry. One Thomas Langford, a former employee of the White Furniture Company, showed how effective this approach was when he criticized union organizers who attacked company president Steve White as a money-grubbing capitalist: "Steve White went duck hunting with the workers," Langford said. "You just don't say those things about a birding buddy."[73]

During the 1970s, unions mounted a last-ditch effort to win workplace union elections in a number of North Carolina factories. Their most notable campaign was an all-or-none election in twenty Drexel Heritage plants in 1970, one that would have led to union representation for all twenty Drexel plants or none at all. This election was one of the largest in the state's furniture industry. A victory in so many plants at one of the state's largest companies might have turned the tide for furniture organizing. But Drexel Heritage workers rejected the union by a twenty-point margin; workers at Henredon and All Wood Products Manufacturing Corp likewise rejected the union.[74] The failure of furniture unions was arguably more pronounced than that of textile unions in the postwar period. In the same year as the All Wood Products union defeat, workers at the J. P. Stevens Textile Mill in Roanoke Rapids won a nationally famous election to unionize the factory, one that became the subject of a feature film (*Norma Rae*).

The 1950s and 1960s saw one of the most consequential shifts in the furniture industry's labor force since its founding: the full inclusion of African American workers. The civil rights movement exploded in the 1950s and 1960s as African Americans protested in mass numbers and governments started passing laws to meet their demands. The 1964 Civil Rights Act banned discrimination on the basis of race in the workplace. Consequently, barriers against African Americans in a number of industries started to crumble. Furniture was no exception.

In fact, researchers saw the North Carolina furniture industry as one of the readiest for desegregation. The furniture industry was located in areas where a considerable number of African Americans lived. Furniture factories still offered a wide variety of unskilled jobs and had a steady demand for labor, as white employees had begun leaving the furniture industry for better-paying, higher-skilled jobs elsewhere. As scholar William E. Fulmer notes: "When the lack of skill barriers is combined with a growing industry, it is inevitable that labor excluded from employment in other industries will find employment in furniture."[75]

The entrance of large companies into the industry also contributed to the diversification of the workforce. New conglomerates hired African Americans both to improve their national image and to please government regulators.[76] These companies had to retain positive relationships with the federal government due to their shareholder obligations as well as their contracts with the federal government. To that end, they had entire departments devoted to hiring and promoting African Americans in order to meet Equal Employment Opportunity Commission regulations.[77]

As a result of these factors, African American employment grew substantially. Fulmer reports that the percentage of African American workers at large firms more than doubled between 1964 and 1969, from approximately 6.4 percent to 13.4 percent of an industry that employed 459,000 workers in 1970.[78] The increase was larger in North Carolina, from 8.7 percent in 1960 to 14.4 percent in 1970. The number of both men and women hired increased, and they were hired for a variety of positions. The number of African American women in the state's furniture industry more than doubled between 1966 and 1970.[79] By 1970, North Carolina had the largest number of African American furniture employees of any state.[80]

Companies also started advertising in African American newspapers. A 1973 Myrtle Desk Company ad for "skilled furniture craftsman and interested trainees," for example, ran in the *Tribunal Aid* newspaper. Thomasville Furniture Industries highlighted Clyde Moore, a new African American supervisor of a factory lumber yard, in a 1979 ad. The ad asserted that at Thomasville, "affirmative action is 'for real' . . . people like Clyde, who have assumed greater career challenges, are helping to make this a better community."[81] Greater African American presence in the industry did not lead to upward mobility, however. In his 1973 report, Fulmer notes that while 7 percent of white employees were managers as of 1970, only 0.7 percent of African American employees in the industry were.[82]

Perhaps the only African American company president in the state industry was David H. Wagner. Born in Davidson County in 1926, Wagner served in the army and became one of the first African Americans to graduate from Wake Forest University School of Law in 1968. At around this time, he embarked on several entrepreneurial ventures. One of these was a furniture factory, the Associated Furniture company, which he founded in 1970.[83] This company had two locations, one in High Point and one in Thomasville, and received a loan from the federal Small Business Administration. In testimony to a U.S. Senate committee, Wagner noted that he needed the loan because his company was attempting to "get off into the area of production which was an area completely new for blacks." The factory had financial problems due to an inability to market its goods. After leadership disputes and a fire, the company folded, and Wagner left the furniture business.[84] He went on to become a successful lawyer and his son-in-law, Harold L. Martin Sr., became president of North Carolina A&T in 2009.

Another leading African American was Charles Scott, a plant manager for U.S. Furniture Industries who traveled frequently and once accompanied the company's president on a trip to Yugoslavia.[85] The influence of Wagner and Scott was fleeting, however. No African American owned a sizable furniture factory in North Carolina in the late 1970s, although one managed a plant in Thomasville from 1972 to 1985.[86] While bleak, the furniture industry was no different in this respect from other state industries. The percentage of African American managers in the textile industry was 0.8 percent in 1970, and there was a comparably minuscule number of Black factory owners.[87]

The new African American employees in the furniture industry were joined by a growing number of women. Women had always played a role in the industry, particularly as seamstresses and secretaries.[88] But in the 1960s, both white and Black women started to take on more operative jobs. They also played a key role in the transportation departments of many factories. Shipping and receiving were similar enough to the secretarial jobs many women had worked before that they could make a seamless transition. As white men moved away from low-wage factory employment in nearly every sector, white and African American women along with African American men started to fill the gap.

These changes did not fix the furniture industry's wage problem. The wage gap between genders and races has shrunk somewhat in recent years, but in the 1970s it was profound. While women currently make about eighty-two cents for every dollar men make, in the 1970s that amount was only fifty-seven to sixty-one cents for every dollar.[89] The amount for African Americans was seventy-three cents for every dollar white workers made in 1980.[90] Because of these wage gaps, more diversity in the industry meant that overall workers' wages stayed low.

In the early 1970s, the North Carolina furniture industry had arguably reached its greatest height. A 1972 report boasted that North Carolina was the leading furniture-producing state in the nation. It was home to sixty-eight thousand furniture-producing employees, nearly twice as many as leading contender California and nearly three times as many as Virginia. North Carolina had 14.1 percent of all furniture-producing employees in the nation and nearly six hundred insured firms, most focused on household furniture.[91] The report documents both North Carolina's dominance and the relative weakness of its competitors. While Virginia prided itself on having the single largest furniture company in the country (Bassett), its towns were too small to compete with the behemoths of High Point and Hickory, and its furniture industry was consequently much smaller.

At the same time North Carolina's furniture industry was hitting its zenith, the midwestern furniture industry was rapidly declining. Michigan, home of Grand Rapids, dropped from the largest furniture-producing state in the early twentieth century to the ninth by 1972. Numerous reasons have been given for this decline, but most center around the slow mechanization of Grand Rapids factories and the focus on high-cost, handmade pieces that could not compete with cheaper southern furniture. The midwestern exposition did not fare much better than the factories. Chicago's furniture market was clearly in decline by the mid-

1970s, and by 1979 the old American Furniture Mart skyscraper had been sold; it was later turned into condos.[92]

In the mid-twentieth century, as it reigned ascendant on the national level, the North Carolina furniture industry expanded its cultural hold on the western Piedmont and mountains, a region increasingly defined by its attachment to furniture factories and associated companies. Companies made their presence felt throughout the community and in the lives of their employees. For example, companies established a network of sports teams for their employees. Tomlinson of High Point fielded baseball, softball, and basketball teams.[93] Other companies that organized baseball, softball, and bowling teams included Alma Desk, Steele, Gilliam, and Howard.[94] Howard's slow pitch softball team was particularly successful, winning the 1973 National Open World Series.[95] These teams built camaraderie within employee ranks and contributed to the generally positive view that many furniture employees had toward their jobs.

Furniture executives also gave back by contributing to the communities they were located in. The most notable example were the Broyhills, who became involved in a wide variety of civic and philanthropic initiatives. Broyhills helped fund the completion of Lenoir's first hospital, the local convention center, a senior center, an events space for the local community college, and two parks. The larger of these parks, the T. H. Broyhill Walking Park, is one of the largest in Caldwell County and has been profiled by local news stations and tourism websites.[96]

The Broyhills were not the only philanthropists in the industry, of course. George Alexander Bernhardt created a local charitable foundation and founded a free medical clinic in the Lenoir area. Several of the buildings on the High Point University campus (like Finch, Hayworth Chapel, and the Plato S. Wilson School of Commerce) were named for their furniture industry benefactors, as well as buildings at Davidson-Davie Community College and Caldwell Community College and Technical Institute.[97]

Furniture intertwined with national culture as well. The biannual Southern Furniture Market was a cultural and social event as well as an economic display. While furniture companies did little to improve the setting of the market during the 1970s—a 1978 article in the *New York*

Times, for example, complained that there were no good restaurants in High Point and nothing to do at night—furniture companies did spend heavily to provide furniture representatives with the best accommodations then available.[98] Furniture salesmen and executives became famous for their ability to wine and dine prospective customers in such a way as to distinguish themselves from the competition.

Celebrities and spectacle also played a role in creating buzz about the event. Furniture executives started associating celebrities with the Southern Furniture Market. Thayer Coggin publicized the fact that football star Joe Namath was a leading purchaser of its products during the fall 1969 market.[99] Douglas Brackett remembered Mickey Mantle at one of his first markets, while Robert Redford attended the fall 1976 market as a guest of Thayer Coggin.[100] The subsidiary High Point Theater began hosting shows by a number of famous performers to coincide with the market as well. These headline names included Dave Brubeck (1975), Dolly Parton (1976), and jazz singer Jeanne Trevor (1977).[101]

The industry began to shrink in the early years of 1970s, however, and by the end of the decade worries over the future of the business were acute. Midcentury growth in most furniture towns slowed as well. Six of the leading furniture towns east and west lost population during the 1970s; Lexington, for example, lost 8.7 percent, while Lenoir lost 6.5 percent. Furniture companies were refusing to innovate. Mergers had led to giant conglomerates that were changing the predominantly local character of the industry. Combined with stagflation and national economic decline, observers worried that the industry was changing for the worse.

But these changes were slow. In 1980, the furniture industry was still a robust third leg of the North Carolina industrial economy. Despite the contraction of the industry, the number of national furniture employees increased by fifty thousand during the 1970s.[102] The U.S. Labor Statistics Bureau reported an employment increase in household furniture of nearly ten thousand and in upholstered furniture of more than three thousand.[103] Furniture towns would remain wedded to the industry for much of the next two decades. But it was already clear by the 1970s that the North Carolina furniture industry's business model was inherently unsustainable and that it might eventually give way.

CHAPTER SIX

Challenges and Resilience

THE FURNITURE INDUSTRY TODAY, 1980–2020

The past forty years have been momentous ones for the North Carolina furniture industry. Since 1980, the industry has reorganized itself completely and taken on a new role in the state's economy. While it lost the preeminent status of a foundational state industry, the furniture sector in North Carolina has by no means disappeared. The 1980s, 1990s, and 2000s were the stretch when furniture companies were faced with ruin and found a new path forward that has allowed them to endure in a modest form to the present day.

The 1980s were prosperous for much of the American economy. Following a Federal Reserve–initiated recession in 1981, the economy as a whole grew steadily throughout the Reagan administration and into the first two years of George H. W. Bush's tenure as president. Consumer spending, business investment, and corporate profits all went up. The greatest beneficiaries of these gains were large, consolidated firms with robust financing and often publicly traded shares. Stock market returns rose approximately 340 percent during the decade, and a number of firms combined and grew as a result of lax regulation, greater access to credit, and sophisticated financial instruments.[1] By the 1980s, much of the furniture industry was now dominated by large companies that were more in touch with national and international financial developments than with specific economic conditions in High Point, Hickory, or Thomasville.

Consequently, the early and mid-1980s seemed like a boom time for the furniture industry in North Carolina. Several new buildings went up, and factories expanded.[2] The biannual furniture markets continued their spectacular success. By 1987, sixteen hundred exhibitors had display space in 150 different buildings in the furniture belt. Companies still projected optimism to newspapers and chased the latest trends, such as the famed Memphis designs from Italy.[3] Furniture wages in the state grew by 70 percent during the 1980s and so did the total number of employees.[4] The height of the industry was in 1990, when it employed ninety-one thousand workers in North Carolina.[5] Most companies believed that any slumps or dips were temporary in nature and connected to the business cycle.[6]

The furniture industry had also begun come to grips with the many regulations imposed by the environmental protection and occupational safety laws of the 1970s. During that decade, there was considerable confusion about how furniture companies would navigate new restrictions on emissions and waste, and rules to ensure the health and safety of its employees. Furniture executives, the vast majority of whom were strident laissez-faire conservatives, worried that they would have to completely reorganize their industry to meet these new government directives.

But the 1980s saw concern about regulations drop precipitously. Even though there was a notable study that linked woodworking to nasal cancer and other respiratory diseases along with repeated long-standing concerns about hearing loss and injuries from machinery, the regulatory environment during the Ronald Reagan and George H. W. Bush administrations was more favorable to industry than that under previous presidents.[7] Enforcement became lax, and furniture executives worried less about the regulatory impact on their business operations. In addition, the industry developed new practices to cope with the federal government's most threatening regulations. Two standard additions to furniture production were dust collectors for woodworking machinery and water-based finishes as opposed to the dangerous, odorous oil-based finishes that had traditionally been used.[8]

The furniture industry also achieved its greatest level of political influence during the 1980s. In 1986, North Carolina senator John P. East committed suicide at the age of fifty-five. Following this tragedy, Governor Jim Martin had the task of picking a replacement to serve out the last four months of East's term. He chose Jim Broyhill, who had been a U.S. House representative from the furniture belt since 1963. Broyhill, once an executive at his father's company, became the highest serving political leader from the furniture industry. His tenure as senator was brief and uneventful, however. He only had time for a few votes, most of which saw him avoiding assuming bold stances on controversial topics.[9]

For Broyhill, 1986 was mostly consumed by the contest for the full senatorial term between himself and former North Carolina governor Terry Sanford. In fact, the main reason that Broyhill was appointed was to give him an incumbent advantage in the November contest.[10] Incumbency was not enough against the experienced, well-liked former governor. Sanford won by more than fifty thousand votes and was sworn in as senator six days later.[11] Broyhill went on to serve as the North Carolina secretary of commerce and has remained a leader and mentor for state Republicans into the 2020s.

The ebullience the industry felt in the early 1980s soon gave way to despair. For one, North Carolina had nearly exhausted its supply of cheap labor in the western areas of the state. With nowhere else to go within the state, companies sent low-wage furniture jobs elsewhere, sometimes to states like Mississippi but often overseas. By 1984, somewhat early in the offshoring process, nearly 20 percent of all American furniture was made overseas in countries such as Taiwan and Hungary.[12]

Loss to foreign competition was exacerbated by the new structure of the industry as a collection of large conglomerates. These entities grew significantly during the 1980s as part of the national mergers and acquisitions boom. Conglomerates took a different approach to economic pressure from the small companies that had previously defined the furniture industry. During the Depression, furniture companies like Broyhill and White Furniture were entirely contained within the community and did whatever they could to stay in business and retain employees.[13] But by the 1980s, a furniture company like Drexel Heritage or Globe-Home was just another line in a ledger sheet. Management in Lancaster or St. Louis did not have any sort of personal attachment to the towns of the North Carolina mountains or Piedmont. Therefore, at the first sign of serious pressure, these factories simply closed and laid off their entire workforces.

The challenges of the 1980s were exacerbated by trade policy shifts in the 1990s. The two most important were the United States' entry into the North American Free Trade Agreement in 1993 and the World Trade Organization in 1995, although the general free trade climate began with Reagan's election in 1981. These new institutions created incentives to offshore American manufacturing. New factories sprang up in China, Mexico, Vietnam, and other countries that paid workers only a fraction of the American minimum wage.

American companies simply could not compete in this new trade environment. Factories started to move overseas and lay off workers. These laid-off factory workers lacked education or training in fields that paid as much as their vanished industrial work. The service jobs that were within their reach paid much less. These changes in trade policy furthered the process of deindustrialization that had begun in the 1970s, leading to public unrest. Ross Perot captured 18.9 percent of the national presidential vote in 1992 based primarily on his opposition to changes in trade policy. As Perot famously explained regarding trade policy with Mexico: "You implement . . . the Mexican trade agreement, where they pay people a dollar an hour, have no health care, no retirement, no pollution controls, . . . and you're going to hear a giant sucking sound of jobs being pulled out of this country."[14] Crime increased in previously bustling urban areas as well. In the middle of the industrial crisis, the national crime rate hit its highest level in 1991 at 758.2 per 100,000 inhabitants, more than double the rate in 2019.[15]

The 1990s and 2000s saw an acceleration of the layoff and closure trend that had begun in the late 1980s. Major factories such as the former Dixie Furniture plant in Lexington, the original Henredon plant in Morganton, and the original Drexel plant closed.[16] Thomasville Furniture Industries was bought and sold several times after 1995 before finally closing all of its Thomasville-based plants in 2014. Heritage Home Group, which at one point owned a number of brands including Broyhill and

Drexel Heritage, filed for bankruptcy in 2018. In 2001, one of the worst years for closures in the furniture belt, twenty-six firms, all of which had more than fifty employees, closed. These firms, located in eighteen different counties in both the eastern and western furniture areas, laid off a total of 3,474 employees.[17]

Challenges in the furniture industry matched those faced by industries across America during this period. Industrial employment began to drop at a precipitous rate. The number of manufacturing employees in the United States dropped from nineteen million in 1979 to sixteen million in 1983, with a further drop to fourteen million by 2004.[18] By 2010, there were fewer manufacturing jobs in the United States than there had been in 1941, when the total American population was nearly a third of its current size. The old industrial centers of the nation hollowed out one by one. Automobile jobs disappeared from Detroit, as did tire jobs from Akron, steel jobs from Pittsburgh, and glass jobs from Toledo.

North Carolina was hit particularly hard by the nation's industrial decline because its industrial system owed its existence to cheap labor.[19] The textile and furniture industries originally came to North Carolina for its lower wages relative to the Northeast and the Midwest. Once companies could find even lower wages, they left en masse. During the worst period of the crisis, from 1990 to 2006, manufacturing jobs in North Carolina dropped from 834,000 to 555,400, a loss of 33 percent.[20] The loss is more profound when one considers the fact that the state's population grew by 21 percent in the first ten years of that period alone. Furniture jobs dropped from a high of nearly ninety thousand in 1990 to just over thirty thousand in 2009.[21] Several furniture towns lost population or had a significant reduction in population growth during this period. Ronda, for example, lost nearly 20 percent of its population in the 1980s, and Statesville lost nearly 6 percent during the same decade. Several of these towns also had significant textile industries that collapsed during this time.

Indeed, the textile exodus was arguably more substantial than the furniture losses. Whereas the furniture industry lost approximately fifty thousand jobs over a fifteen-year period, the textile industry lost a hundred thousand jobs in only a five-year period.[22] While towns like Hudson and Lenoir struggled in the furniture belt, Kannapolis and Burlington suffered similar challenges in the textile region. Tobacco was also devastated by both trade changes and shifting attitudes in public health. The Tobacco Master Settlement Agreement, reached in 1998 with nearly every state attorney general, cost companies more than $365 billion. By the end of the 1990s, the tobacco industry was devastated. Thousands of tobacco had workers lost their jobs, Durham and Winston-Salem had suffered years-long declines, and several eastern tobacco towns had nearly fallen off the map.

It is tempting to view these closings as natural statistical developments that reflect the change from an industrial to a service economy. In fact, the population of many North Carolina furniture towns grew at the same time that their factories closed. But the closures of the North Carolina furniture belt constituted a human tragedy that devastated thousands of lives. The book *Closing* chronicles the shutdown of White Furniture Company in 1993. After over a hundred years in business, the White family sold the company to Hickory Manufacturing, which managed it poorly for several years before shutting it down for good in 1993.

News of the closure shocked the many employees at the Mebane factory. Worker Annette Foust Patterson recalled that when the mill closed, "A sadness come over everybody's face like, 'What are we going to do now?' . . . you could see the hurt."[23] Authors Bill Bamberger and Cathy Davidson note that the most consistent theme among the former employees they interviewed regarding the closure was the personal attachment to the company: "They viewed the company as an extension of themselves—and vice versa. Closing down the factory, they felt as if their lives were closing down. . . . Overstocked parts such as chair legs or drawers were also burned up. What wasn't useful was discarded—and that's how the workers felt about themselves."[24]

The story at White Furniture Company was repeated countless times in other furniture towns. Stanley Furniture's plant in Robbinsville was the last factory in Graham County. When it closed in 2014, local Patricia Stratton lamented, "If somebody doesn't open it back up and getting some jobs in there, I'm afraid this town will kind of die off."[25] Many of these towns were not able to find another economic base. They became mainly bedroom communities for larger surrounding towns that embraced the newer banking and technology fields. Several Piedmont furniture towns benefited from growth in Greensboro and Winston-Salem, while western towns had connections to the prosperous technology town of Hickory.

Along with many towns, some of the populations affected by plant shutdowns have not recovered either. By the 1980s and 1990s, furniture companies had finally begun to fully include women and African Americans in their workforces. Both groups started to move up in companies, and their pay rates improved as well. But just as many were about to move into the highest-paying and most successful positions, offshoring swept away those positions and the companies that African American men and women worked for. The workers profiled in *Closing* speak to this loss. Annette Foust Patterson was an African American woman who had achieved a position in the traditionally male rough mill.[26] Robert Riley had become the first African American supervisor at White Furniture before the plant closure. Both Riley and Patterson were forced into more menial jobs with lower pay and more precarious work conditions after the plant closed.[27]

High Point did not suffer the same fate. It survived and even thrived because it embodied the new service economy. Designers, photographers, printers, educators, truckers, and lighting experts in the town served the furniture manufacturing industry.[28] But more importantly, High Point became a town devoted to a great service event: the biannual market. The factories and businesses of downtown High Point were almost all converted to furniture showrooms or offices for companies associated with the market. This showroom supply was soon met by demand. In 1995, just under seventy thousand people visited sixteen hundred exhibitors at what was by then known as the International Home Furnishings Market.[29] By 2004, there were more than seventy-five thousand visitors, and the number of exhibitors skyrocketed to over three thousand.[30] Market organizers also continued to invite celebrities. A 2004 article listed famous people who had been seen at the market: "home decorating diva (and convicted felon) Martha Stewart, screen 'icon' Lauren Bacall, fashion designer and MTV host Todd Oldham[,] . . . golf legend Arnold Palmer[,] . . . former supermodel Kathy Ireland, former NFL great John Elway and former NASCAR driver Richard Petty."[31]

Although it took manufacturing jobs away, globalization was a boon to the furniture industry. It was during the 1980s and 1990s that the International Home Furnishings Market became more of an international affair. Early international visitors from countries such as Canada and the United Kingdom were eventually joined by others from all over the world, all of whom flocked to High Point to view the latest trends and conduct business transactions. In 2004, 110 countries were represented at the market.[32] The closures in the state's western furniture industry meant there was less competition from rival expositions. Previously, High Point had competed with the showrooms of Lenoir, Drexel, and Hickory, which displayed their goods during the biannual markets. But with most of those factories closed, High Point reigned supreme.

Visitor numbers grew slightly throughout the 2000s and 2010s. The number as of 2019 was between seventy-five thousand and eighty thousand. But the economic impact has only continued to grow as more companies open to service the market as designers, showroom specialists, and facilitators of events. Tens of thousands of jobs in North Carolina and the furniture-producing areas of southern Virginia have been tied to the market. Between 2004 and 2013, the economic impact of the market grew from approximately $1 billion to $5.39 billion, an amount that jumped to $6.73 billion in 2019.[33]

While many furniture facilities closed in North Carolina in the 1990s and 2000s, High Point's buildings expanded. One early example of the shift toward showrooms in High Point was the 1982 construction of Market Square, a furniture center and showroom housed within the former Tomlinson Chair Manufacturing Company complex. During the next decade, High Point added 3,000,000 feet of display space, including a 183-foot-tall tower addition to Market Square. The 2000s saw the formation of the High Point International Home Furnishings Market Authority, a new organization that began coordinating the entire market.[34] There was also construction of the eighty-five-foot-tall Plaza Suites and the Showplace, a strikingly modern glass building that serves as a welcome area for what is now called the High Point Market.

These successes highlight the disconnect between the experience at the High Point Market and in the rest of the manufacturing centers of the state. Karla Jones, executive director of the Bienenstock Furniture Library, once worked for a company that handled publicity and advertising for Thomasville Furniture Industries. Her responsibility was to prepare press kits for media representatives so they could display the newest lines in newspaper and magazine advertisements after the market. She noted in a 2022 interview that while "the factories were closing," the designers, purchasers, and showroom employees were left relatively unscathed: "At the market, it did not feel as though anything had happened." However, after the recession of the early 2000s, furniture companies sharply reduced their spending on market visitors and press kits.[35]

The unique role of the market in the industry has also led to a change in the built environment within High Point itself. High Point's downtown has undergone a peculiar change since the 1960s. Its retail businesses, department stores, and many of its shops have left for the suburbs, as they have in many other downtowns. But unlike other cities whose downtowns struggled until recently, few of High Point's storefronts are truly empty, even when nothing appears to be happening in them. High Point is what John Joe Schlichtman refers to as "temp town"; its storefronts are simply closed to the public while professionals clean, arrange, and prepare for the next market event. He notes that "the buildings of High Point's downtown, stages that are spotlighted twice each year, are in constant preparation for the big productions in the five-month periods that precede each Market."[36] Schlichtman cites the remarkable statistic that even as its storefronts looked abandoned, the amount of furniture showroom space in High Point increased from six hundred thousand square feet in 1963 to approximately twelve million square feet in 2003.[37]

The market, and the businesses called in to prepare for it, brings in tax revenue and allows the town to handle the influx of visitors every

April and October. But it leaves High Point without the restaurants, coffee shops, and bookstores that have revitalized downtowns in Durham, Winston-Salem, and Greensboro. High Point has sacrificed its downtown vitality for the market and all of the business associated with it. Residents have been forced to give up the amenities of other cities for a biannual event that many of them will never be able to visit. (In fact, they have often been advised to avoid celebrity chasing and going downtown during the market.)[38] Only in the past five to ten years, with the help of High Point University and its significant customer base, has downtown High Point started to embrace such amenities. It now has a coffee shop, a bookstore, and several restaurants, and the closure of Oak Hollow Mall in 2017 has created even more room for retail operations to open up downtown.

Outside of general growth in High Point, the trends that characterized the furniture decline of the 1980s and 1990s have continued to the present day. American firms simply cannot compete on price alone with countries such as China and Vietnam that have drastically lower labor costs. This dynamic is particularly apparent in the case goods industry. Low- and medium-grade case goods manufacturers in North Carolina continue to close and ship their factories overseas. The Stanley Furniture factory in Robbinsville closed in 2014, while the Hickory Springs Manufacturing plant in Micaville closed in 2020.[39]

A few companies have tried to fight back against offshoring and takeover by foreign companies. The most famous fight was launched by Bassett Furniture in Virginia, the subject of Beth Macy's 2014 book *Factory Man*. In the early 2000s, John D. Bassett III launched a legal crusade in the World Trade Organization against unfair trade practices by China— its stealing of intellectual property and its flooding the market with cheap goods—that were devastating American furniture manufacturers. Bassett enlisted the help of numerous North Carolina manufacturers in his crusade. These manufacturers ended up securing millions in trade duties from China to help keep their factories open in Virginia, North Carolina, and other furniture-producing states.[40]

But North Carolina furniture has also found a way to stay viable outside of the world of cheap competition and trade wars. Higher-end manufacturing companies such as Thayer Coggin and Century Furniture embrace design and customization instead of trying to compete by producing cheaper, mass-produced pieces. Foreign manufacturers often produce in bulk to reduce their interocean shipping costs. But it is hard to produce upholstered pieces that may have little in common with one another in bulk.[41] Higher-end furniture companies have created a niche in the face of this shortcoming and now offer dozens of different colors, designs, trims, fabrics, and design components. They use in-house designers to craft unique options and work with local suppliers whenever they can.

According to some current manufacturers, this approach has allowed furniture companies to overcome international competition and even thrive. After twenty years of general decline, the furniture industry added a modest number of jobs in the 2010s, and North Carolina remains the furniture manufacturing capital of the United States.[42] As of 2022, dozens of furniture companies, including case goods and upholstered furniture companies located in the furniture belt and beyond, were listed in a directory of manufacturers based in North Carolina.[43]

In certain ways, the furniture industry has not changed over the past three decades. It continues to be wary of automation, as the history of the factories of Tomlinson Companies suggests. Tomlinson is still in business manufacturing high-end furniture in the state. At its Thomasville Erwin-Lambeth factory location, much of the technology in use has not changed in decades. While it uses a computer numerical control router for cutting basic forms out of wood and some other computerized machines and components, computers are vastly outnumbered by traditional machines such as band saws and steam presses.[44] Employees staple webbing onto sofas and chairs and sew and cut out fabric almost entirely by hand. The shipping and receiving departments and the warehouse also operate much as they did decades ago. There are no robots or interconnected automated procedures like one would see at a modern car or computer components factory. The amount of human labor is remarkable for factories in the twenty-first century that produce at the high volume of a factory like Tomlinson Erwin-Lambeth.[45]

Retail has been an area of success along with more niche manufacturing. One of the most significant retail developments in the industry is Furnitureland South. Founded in 1969, Furnitureland moved to its flagship store on the business loop of I-85 in 1990. That store is the largest retail furniture store in the country. It was expanded numerous times in the 1990s and 2000s and is now an anchor for a row of furniture-related businesses. This retail outlet serves as a counterpoint to the showrooms of downtown High Point, which are mostly restricted to members of the industry and closed to the public.

A writer for the *New York Times* described Furnitureland South's business approach in 1985: "The front areas of the store are filled with furniture, attractively grouped and accessorized; however some corners have never seen a designer's hand, with sofas and tables placed close together in rows. However the selling floor accounts for only a portion of the store's volume. Salesclerks are constantly being paged to handle customers on the toll-free number, quoting prices on model numbers and sending them brochures and fabric swatches." Further, according to the article, retailers like Furnitureland South "sell first-quality furniture at discounts of 35 to 50 percent off the manufacturer's suggested retail prices."[46] By 2019, over sixty thousand visitors were shopping at Furnitureland South every year.[47] In order to emphasize its impact, in 1998 Furnitureland South produced an eighty-five-foot-tall highboy, which was taller than both High Point's chest of drawers and Thomasville's chair.

The Hickory Furniture Mart has followed a similar path as Furnitureland South. For the first two decades of its existence, it was an extension of the smaller showrooms that dotted the furniture belt and operated alongside the primary Southern Furniture Market in High Point. But during the 1980s, major factories began to close their own showrooms and focus on High Point. The year 1985 marked a turning point with the departure of Bassett Furniture from the market in Hickory.[48] With the wholesale market concentrated in High Point, the Hickory Furniture Mart began to cater to retail customers. It was enormously successful, expanding numerous times over the next three decades and rivaling Furnitureland South in size and attention. It received national attention in

1998 when designer Christopher Lowell glowingly reviewed several of its showrooms on the Discovery Channel.[49] This relationship with home design television, one of the fastest growing genres of cable television, has paid dividends for the industry in the two decades since Lowell's reviews.[50]

Design is another component of the furniture industry that cannot be easily exported. North Carolina currently has dozens of design firms both large and small. They use state-of-the-art design technology and often work within large furniture firms. Several designers have moved away from residential furniture and focus instead on contract furniture for schools, businesses, and government organizations. Designers make pieces both for the biannual markets and for newer stores throughout the state that are open year-round.[51] A 2007 study tallied sixty-one furniture design companies with 252 employees, a number that has certainly increased in recent years as the industry has grown.[52]

Carol Gregg and David Williams, designers working in the Piedmont, epitomize different approaches to the work of furniture design in the twenty-first century. Gregg is the founder of red egg, a furniture design company that produces home furniture inspired by a trip Gregg made to China's antique furniture warehouses. Red egg, which produces what Gregg describes her as "fresh, fun, quirky," "Asian inspired furniture with a twist," began in San Francisco but moved to High Point in 2004.[53] Gregg's showroom is now located in a historic High Point home and is a popular attraction at the market.

Williams, on the other hand, focuses on contract furniture. This field is entirely divorced from the High Point Market and the rest of the home furnishings sphere. He designs pieces for libraries (for example, the library at West Point), hospitals, and major events from his studio in Thomasville. His work is inspired by both neoclassical masters and modernist architects such as Ludwig Mies van der Rohe and Le Corbusier. Both architects lent their aesthetic vision to modernist furniture design, with Mies devising one of the most famous chair designs of the twentieth century, the Barcelona chair.[54]

One of Williams's most recent creations is emblematic of his career and development. Wingding, a chair designed for Trinity Furniture, has the curvilinear forms and modernist approach that are typical of Williams's work. It has an advanced plywood design that molds around the user and provides privacy in spaces such as libraries. Wingding is also an example of furniture design incorporating new technology. It has charging outlets that allow users to work at laptops while sitting in the chair. Williams remarked in a 2022 interview that the technology used at nearly every step of the Wingding construction process, from the plywood used to the electronic components, did not exist ten years ago.

Local institutions have also played a role in keeping the furniture industry viable. Traditional and community colleges continue to expand their course offerings and connections with the furniture industry. After years of decline, the furniture program at North Carolina State University has been revived over the past ten years. The university still has a minor in furniture manufacturing as well as a furniture testing facility at the Center for Additive Manufacturing and Logistics, which works closely with companies to test their materials and products.[55] Other four-year universities with furniture-related interior design programs include the University of North Carolina at Greensboro, Appalachian State University, and Western Carolina University.[56]

The relationship between companies and community colleges was highlighted in 2014 with the opening of the Catawba Valley Furniture Academy at Catawba Valley Community College. In addition to offering classes, the academy provides training for specific positions and has a simulated factory and showroom.[57] Caldwell Community College and Technical Institute has a similar furniture factory lab that was created in collaboration with four local furniture companies. The lab contains a simulated factory and offers intensive programs in upholstery and furniture sewing.[58]

High Point University is another success story in the region from the past three decades. The school was founded as High Point College in 1924 and had fewer than fifteen hundred students at a time over the course of its first ninety-one years of operation. In 1981, the college graduated its first furniture marketing bachelor's students.[59] Its growth accelerated immensely beginning in 2005, when renowned businessman and public speaker Nido Qubein became president and committed to turning it into a "life skills university." Some of those skills have included furniture design and marketing.

High Point University currently has a department of home furnishings and interior design through which students can earn an interior design degree as well as a sales major with a concentration in furniture. The department offers ten courses related to furnishings and that cover fields from branding and marketing to the attributes of classically designed interiors.[60] High Point University students receive hands-on experience at the market and have been hired by numerous companies through connections made there.[61]

These new designers and college graduates have begun to work with a new labor force. Latino immigrants have moved into the traditional furniture belt region of the state, rapidly becoming one of the largest ethnic groups in North Carolina. They are a considerable presence in Burke County, where they have entered the furniture industry in addition to the chicken processing industry.[62] Hannah Gill and others have argued that they helped address the labor shortages of 1990s and 2000s, taking up loud, dust-filled, hot, and dangerous positions that are essential to so many aspects of furniture manufacture even in the twenty-first century.[63] These immigrants replace the women and African Americans of earlier years who have left the industry for arguably more physically comfortable positions. In a 2004 article for the University of North Carolina research magazine *Endeavors*, professor Meenu Tewari describes this trend: "This change in the workforce began in the early nineties, partly because of efforts by local officials to attract other types of businesses to the High Point region. Young residents were drawn away from furniture factories and into slightly higher-paying office jobs, and some furniture companies actually faced a tight labor market." A worker at Bernhardt Furniture whom Tewari interviewed noted that "Hispanic immigrants were not taking jobs away from residents; they were reducing an overwhelming work load."[64]

Vietnamese and Hmong immigrants have also become a significant force. These men and women fled southeast Asia following the Vietnam War. Many thousands of them settled in North Carolina, particularly in the western counties. Hmong and Vietnamese immigrants, like Latino immigrants, have been able to fill labor shortages in areas that have re-quired low-wage and repetitive work. Clyde Hooker, the president of a Virginia factory with plants in North Carolina, reported in a 1999 inter-view that one of his Greensboro plants had hired between fifty and sixty Vietnamese immigrants. He praised these employees and noted that they were "some of the best workers that we have."[65] Through this effort, they have become pivotal members of the modern North Carolina furni-ture industry.

Community colleges and remaining furniture factories, along with tech companies and ambitious real estate developers, have led to a re-vitalization of the furniture region.[66] Historic furniture towns such as Statesville, Conover, and Boone have all seen their populations increase by more than 15 percent over the past two decades, while Hickory's has grown by 16 percent since 2000. Hickory has also developed a robust technology sector, and even became a contestant in Amazon's second headquarters competition in 2017 and 2018.[67] Thomasville has grown by more than 30 percent in the past two decades. It has continued to fund its furniture sector, foster a relationship with furniture and the local community college, and find new tenants for its previously empty build-ings, such as the sprawling Thomasville Emporium that replaced an old Belk store.[68] Lexington still has three furniture factories as of 2021 and has also become a tourist hub as the capital of western North Carolina barbecue.[69] These cities have been successful while still maintaining a siz-able furniture sector.

The 1980s and 1990s were world changing for the North Carolina fur-niture industry. Like tobacco and textiles, furniture lost its status as a foundational state industry, to be replaced by banking, technology, and health care. But loss of status did not mean that the furniture industry became a historical relic. Instead, it improvised and innovated. Furni-ture companies spent years searching for business models that worked. They forged new relationships with local institutions and even started working with foreign companies. Through this effort, the North Carolina furniture industry has outlived predictions of its imminent demise and continues to be a strong contributor to the society, economy, and inter-national reputation of the Old North State.

COVID-19 and the Furniture Industry

The COVID-19 pandemic has had a devastating impact on nearly every sector of the global economy. As for the North Carolina furniture industry, the effects have been mixed. The High Point Market was hit especially hard. As an indoor gathering of thousands of people packed closely together, it was particularly susceptible to governmental regulation and visitor apprehension. In spring 2020, the market was canceled for the first time since the Second World War.[1]

Subsequent markets were more limited affairs. Approximately forty-one thousand people attended the nine-day fall 2020 show, a significant drop-off from the 2019 number of seventy-five thousand in one week.[2] The reason for the longer runtime was that organizers wanted to spread out participants and reduce crowding at each facility. A mask mandate was in place, and there were no notable public health problems related to the event. By fall 2021, vaccines and relaxed government mandates resulted in growing attendance numbers and a returning sense of normalcy to that year's fall market.[3]

In other areas, the pandemic may have reversed trends in the furniture industry that stretch back at least four decades. Labor costs have always been the major determining factor for where factories are located and how they operate. Domestic companies simply could not compete with labor costs in other countries. But since early 2020, basic labor costs have been less important than they have ever were. Material and shipping costs have increased more than the cost of wages in the United States. One of the leading news stories of 2021 was the backup of container ships and trucks at ports, most notably the port in Los Angeles. Many of these costs can be avoided with domestic manufacturing.

This significant shift has led to renewed attention on the North Carolina furniture industry. Furniture did not fall in the 1990s and 2000s as far as tobacco and textiles. Its ability to withstand changes in consumer taste and develop a niche market over the past two decades gave it a substantial manufacturing base. This base provided an opportunity in the era of supply chain failures and labor shutdowns abroad that is supported by a growing interest in home design from online sources, social media trends, and the continuing popularity of home design television.

Drawing on statistics and interviews with furniture executives and community college students, a November 2021 *New York Times* in November 2021 offers a rosy picture of the furniture industry: "More than a year [into the pandemic], the furniture companies that dot Hickory, N.C., in the foothills of the Blue Ridge Mountains, have been presented with an unforeseen opportunity: The pandemic and its ensuing supply chain disruptions have dealt a setback to the factories in China and southeast Asia that decimated American manufacturing in the 1980s and 1990s with cheaper imports."[4]

The pandemic has boosted the hopes of manufacturers. Century Furniture CEO Alex Shuford III believes that the market could support a substantial growth in upholstered goods and the kinds of factories that survived the 2010s. Textile companies that have worked closely with upholstered furniture companies continue to succeed. Community colleges have preserved their connections to manufacturing even as enrollment has declined overall. Bolstered by these prospects, Coley Home announced a new facility in Claremont in November 2021, and less than a month later Sherrill Furniture announced plans to build a new $2.9 million factory and create ninety jobs in Conover.[5]

Even with these benefits, the pandemic has been a drain on the furniture industry as on so many others. Furniture factories continue to have problems attracting talented, committed industrial labor. As the *New York Times* article notes, "Employees at Century have been working overtime to catch up with the backlog, but workers burn out, and furniture margins are so thin that paying overtime labor rates can eat into profits."[6] The cycle of labor shortages, demand fluctuations, and new COVID-19 variants has created uncertainty in manufacturing. In the twenty-first century, factories require millions of dollars in capital and a guarantee that an initial investment in buildings and high-tech machinery will pay off in the long term. With the prospect of vaccines and acquired immunity potentially blunting the impact of the virus, many companies are still hesitant to fully invest the money required to build substantial new factories and take advantage of pandemic-related opportunities.

The 2020s may end up being as defining as the 1990s were for the North Carolina furniture industry. Time will tell if pandemic-induced supply constraints will continue to bolster the state's manufacturing prospects. But as in earlier times, North Carolina currently has an abundance of raw materials, a large labor source, an international service-based event in the High Point Market, and insightful leaders such as Shuford and George Alexander Bernhardt who have a vision for the industry's future. In light of these factors, there is no doubt that the furniture industry will survive this tumultuous period and continue to prosper for the foreseeable future.

APPENDIX

COMPANY	YEAR FOUNDED	LOCATION
Alma Furniture Company	1895	High Point
Bassett Furniture	1902	Bassett, Virginia
Bernhardt Furniture	1889	Lenoir
Broyhill	1941	Lenoir
Century Furniture	1947	Hickory
Dixie Furniture	1901	Lexington
Drexel Furniture Company; it became Drexel Enterprises in 1960 and then Drexel Heritage after its acquisition by U.S. Plywood-Champion Papers in 1968	1903	Drexel
Eagle Furniture Company	1893	High Point
Erwin-Lambeth (run by Katherine Lambeth); it became a division of Tomlinson Companies and is now Tomlinson Erwin-Lambeth	1898	Thomasville
Globe Furniture Company (merged with Home Furniture Company in 1902)	1896	High Point
Globe-Home Furniture Company (created by merger of Globe and Home Furniture Companies)	1902	High Point
Greensboro Furniture Company (closed 1915)	1890	Greensboro
Henredon	1945	Morganton
Hickory Springs Manufacturing	1944	Hickory
High Point Furniture Company	1889	High Point
High Point Mantel and Table Company	1900	High Point
Lenoir Furniture Company (founded by J. M. Bernhardt)	1889	Lenoir

COMPANY	YEAR FOUNDED	LOCATION
Myrtle Desk Company (started by the founder of Alma Furniture Company)	1899	High Point
Stanley Furniture	1924	Stanleytown, Virginia, as well as High Point; the factory was in Robbinsville
Thayer Coggin	1953	High Point
Thomasville Chair Company; it became Thomasville Furniture Industries in 1961	1904	Thomasville
Tomlinson Chair Manufacturing Company; it was renamed Tomlinson of High Point in 1934 and is now Tomlinson Companies	1900	High Point
White Furniture Company	1881	Mebane

1. Ready, *Tar Heel State*, 200.

2. The absence of a published, full-length history of the North Carolina furniture industry is remarkable. The two most cited sources are William Stevens's *Anvil of Adversity* (1968) and David N. Thomas's 1964 PhD dissertation, "Early History of the North Carolina Furniture Industry, 1880–1921." Stevens's book is a biography of a furniture executive written by the vice president of that executive's company, making it a decidedly partial source. Thomas's work, which was never published, has been cited in numerous reports and prominent history books. Other theses and dissertations have dealt with the industry in chapters or with specific aspects such as health and safety. See Goldsmith, "Respiratory Disease," Medearis, "Furniture Industry," and Selby, "Industrial Growth." Most books pertaining to the furniture industry in general, furthermore, deal with a particular company or time period. See Macy, *Factory Man* (about Bassett Furniture in Virginia, although it contains a few sections on the industry in North Carolina); Bamberger and Davidson, *Closing* (about the White Furniture Company); Harden, *Boling*; and Huffman, *Drexel Enterprises*.

This lack of material is referred to in a report in the George Antone Furniture Industry Research Papers (1885–1993) in the special collections of Appalachian State University Library in Boone. The report details an attempted history of the western North Carolina furniture industry and lists the numerous challenges that the researchers had faced: "primary and secondary resources are few," "archival information was not preserved," "a number of abortive efforts resembling this project have failed," and analyzing "the most helpful sources . . . is time-consuming and tedious." Antone's project never led to a published product.

3. In *Anvil of Adversity*, Stevens refers to the furniture belt as a figure eight of highways stretching from High Point to Morganton (55–57). Although I rely on this definition, his belt does not take into consideration a number of plants that were important to the history of the state's furniture industry, such as White Furniture Company in Mebane and Cranford Furniture in Asheboro.

4. A sizable number of historical works have been written specifically about these figures. For more on Ella Mae Wiggins, see Huber, "Mill Mother's Lament." Cannon's definitive biography is Vanderburg's *Cannon Mills and Kannapolis*. For more on Page and the fight against pellagra, see Cooper, *Walter Hines Page*.

5. The connection between furniture and textile workers is one of the few topics that have yielded significant historical studies into the industry. See Selby, "'Better to Starve.'"

6. For the importance of *Like a Family*, see the reviews by Gavin Wright and Joan W. Scott as well as "History Headlines," Larson, "Potential, Potential, Potential," and Berlin, "A Benevolent and Brutal Paternalism."

7. Glass, *Textile Industry in North Carolina*, xiii.

8. O'Hanlon, "5,350 Companies."

1. Korstian, *Economic Development of the Furniture Industry*, 8.

2. Hergesheimer, *Map*.

3. Francis Nicholson to Henderson Walker, November 8, 1699, in Saunders, *Colonial Records of North Carolina*, 1:514–15.

4. Tryon Palace, "Furniture Collection."

5. Bivins, *Furniture of Coastal North Carolina*, 63.

6. Bivins, *Furniture of Coastal North Carolina*, 61–64.

7. Bivins, *Furniture of Coastal North Carolina*, 61.

8. Perquimans Precinct Court minutes, August 7–8, 1693, in Saunders, *Colonial Records of North Carolina*, 1:398.

9. North Carolina Governor's Council minutes, May 8, 1713, in Saunders, *Colonial Records of North Carolina*, 2:42.

10. Bivins, *Furniture of Coastal North Carolina*, 69.

11. Segal, "How to Identify."

12. Alexander Crane, *North Carolina Furniture of the Coastal Plain, 1685–1835*, unpublished manuscript, in Alexander Crane Collection.

13. Alexander Crane, "North Carolina Furniture as Listed in 'Southern Antiques,'" in Alexander Crane Collection.

14. Salem Board minutes, 1812, in Fries, *Records of the Moravians*, 7:3171.

15. Salem Board minutes, 1825, in Fries and Rights, *Records of the Moravians*, 8:3741. Wohlfahrt was related to the famed Moravian painter who anglicized his name to Daniel Welfare.

16. Salem Board minutes, in Fries, *Records of the Moravians*, 7:3266.

17. F. W. Marshall to the Unity Elders Conference, July 1786, in Fries, *Records of the Moravians*, 5:2148.

18. Bivins, *Furniture of Coastal North Carolina*, 51–53.

19. City of Winston-Salem, "Town of Salem."

20. *Manufactures of the United States in 1860*, 420–38.

21. Bond, "Cabinet-Making."

22. "Museum Motifs," 157; Bivins, *Furniture of Coastal North Carolina*, 55.

23. Bivins, *Furniture of Coastal North Carolina*, 268.

24. Bivins, *Furniture of Coastal North Carolina*, 507–8.

25. Marshall and Leimenstoll, *Thomas Day*, 45–47.

26. For more on the legacy of furniture manufacturing in eastern towns, see Bivins, *Furniture of Coastal North Carolina*, 57.

27. Pinchbeck, *Virginia Negro Artisan*, 33.

28. Genovese, *Roll, Jordan, Roll*, 531.

29. Byrne, "The Hiring of Woodson," 255.

30. Byrne, "The Hiring of Woodson," 255.

31. Franklin, *Free Negro in North Carolina*, 228.

32. Franklin, *Free Negro in North Carolina*, 228.

33. Marshall and Leimenstoll, *Thomas Day*, 14.

34. Marshall and Leimenstoll, *Thomas Day*, 16.

35. Marshall and Leimenstoll, *Thomas Day*, 45.

36. Marshall and Leimenstoll, *Thomas Day*, 83.

37. Marshall and Leimenstoll, *Thomas Day*, 84.

38. Marshall and Leimenstoll, *Thomas Day*, 55.

39. Marshall and Leimenstoll, *Thomas Day*, 56.

40. Marshall and Leimenstoll, *Thomas Day*, 58.

41. *Journals of Senate and House of Commons*, 238.

42. Franklin, *Free Negro in North Carolina*, 45.

43. Marshall and Leimenstoll, *Thomas Day*, 29.

44. Marshall and Leimenstoll, *Thomas Day*, 22.

45. Franklin, *Free Negro in North Carolina*, 160.

46. Marshall and Leimenstoll, *Thomas Day*, 27.

47. Bachynski, "American Medicine"; Finkelman, "America's 'Great Chief Justice'"; Clayton, "E. A. Poe."

48. Moonan, "Antiques"; Ketchum, *American Cabinetmakers*, 332.

49. Rauschenberg, "A Study," 41–46.

50. *Manufactures of the United States in 1860*, 420–38.

51. Hazzard, *New Map*.

52. Barrett, *Civil War*, 360.

53. Barrett, *Civil War*, 355.

CHAPTER 2. A FURNITURE BOOM

1. Waggoner, "N.C. Revises."

2. Carron, *Grand Rapids Furniture*, 33–38.

3. Carron, *Grand Rapids Furniture*, 39.

4. *White Directory*, 122–26.

5. Woodward, *Origins of the New South*, 118–20.

6. Stoesen, *Guilford County*, 16–17.

7. *Branson's North Carolina Business Directory*, 69–72.

8. High Point Chamber of Commerce, *Building and Builders*, 96–97.

9. Darr and Little, "West High Street Historic District."

10. Ebert, "High Point's Evolution," 52.

11. Farriss, *High Point, N.C.* (1900), 20, 61, 45.

12. Thomas, "Getting Started," 26.

13. Farriss, *High Point, N.C.* (1900), 42, 85, 81, 53.

14. Lowry, "Beginnings," 124.

15. High Point Furniture Company, *Six Great Leaders*.

16. Bishop Furniture Company, catalog, 25.

17. Ransom, *City Built on Wood*, 31.

18. Sanborn Map Company, "High Point, Guilford Co., North Carolina, January 1902," in North Carolina Maps.

19. E. Leroy Briggs, interview, February 7, 2008, in American Furniture Hall of Fame Oral Histories.

20. Andreas, *Cook County, Illinois*, 623–24.

21. *North Carolina Year Book* (1903), 287–91.

22. Farriss, *High Point, N.C.* (1896), 2.

23. Farriss, *High Point, N.C.* (1896), 3.

24. Farriss, *High Point, N.C.* (1896), 7.

25. "High Point."

26. "Messenger Bureau."

27. "Southern Furniture Manufacturing."

28. Thomas, "Early History," 14.

29. Hall, Leloudis, Korstad, Murphy, Jones, and Daly, *Like a Family*, 51–56, 68.

30. N.C. Department of Labor Statistics, *Eleventh Annual Report*, 138; Ransom, *City Built on Wood*, 39.

31. N.C. Bureau of Labor Statistics, *Fourth Annual Report*, 148.

32. N.C. General Assembly, *Laws and Resolutions*, 773; "Furniture"; "Morganton."

33. N.C. Department of Labor Statistics, *Twelfth Annual Report,* 63; Stevens, *Anvil of Adversity*, 50, 61.

34. "Notice of Incorporation"; N.C. Department of Labor Statistics, *Eleventh Annual Report*, 140.

35. William P. Kemp Sr., interview by John Tobin, December 14, 1988, in American Furniture Hall of Fame Oral Histories.

36. "Goldsboro's Growth."

37. "Goldsboro Gossip."

38. N.C. Bureau of Labor Statistics, *Ninth Annual Report*, 286.

39. Stevens, *Anvil of Adversity*, 49–50.

40. Stevens, *Anvil of Adversity*, 63–65.

41. The Thomasville chair plant was a small handicraft shop that J. L. Oliver represented as the origin of the state's furniture industry. This shop, opened in 1854 according to Oliver, began as a small operation that was virtually indistinguishable from earlier cabinetmaking shops and is therefore not usually considered the beginning of the modern industry. See Oliver, *Development and Structure*, 92. The question of which was truly the first furniture factory in North Carolina is still debated. As David Nolan Thomas notes, "the transition in furniture making from cabinet-shops to manufacturing plants was usually so gradual that it was often not clear how a given establishment should be classified" ("Early History," 7).

42. *White Directory*, 254.

43. *White Directory*, 252.

44. Bamberger and Davidson, *Closing*, 27.

45. White Furniture Company, *From Generation to Generation*.

46. CPI Inflation Calculator, https://www.officialdata.org/us/inflation/1900?endYear=1914&amount=8; White Furniture Company, *34 Years at It*.

47. White Furniture Company, *34 Years at It*.

48. "North Carolina" in U.S. Census Bureau, *Twelfth Census of the United States*, 665–68.

CHAPTER 3. GROWTH AND EXPANSION

1. U.S. Census Bureau, *Twelfth Census of the United States*, 661.

2. U.S. Census Bureau, *Twelfth Census of the United States*, 661.

3. Small, "State of North Carolina."

4. Farriss, *High Point, North Carolina*, 55.

5. Whittington and Hoover, *High Point, North Carolina*, 62–63.

6. Whittington and Hoover, *High Point, North Carolina*, 53–54.

7. U.S. Census Bureau, *Fourteenth Census of the United States*, 128.

8. Fulmer, *Negro in the Furniture Industry*, 7–11.

9. "Southern Furniture Manufacturing"; *High Point, North Carolina, City Directory*; *North Carolina Year Book* (1916), 205–6, 274; *North Carolina Year Book* (1904), 296.

10. U.S. Census Bureau, *Fourteenth Census of the United States*, 8, 22–24.

11. Darr and Little, "West High Street Historic District," 2, 15.

12. Thomas, "Getting Started," 26.

13. Whittington and Hoover, *High Point, North Carolina*, 60.

14. Whittington and Hoover, *High Point, North Carolina*, 159.

15. Whittington and Hoover, *High Point, North Carolina*, 161, 75.

16. Idol, "High Pointer."

17. "To Make Iron Beds."

18. Brown, "High Point."

19. "Municipal Elections."

20. "Sketch."

21. Steelman, "Republicanism in North Carolina," 153–68.

22. "Justice's Weekly Letter."

23. "Mr. Cox Welcomed Home."

24. Sam White to J. Elwood Cox, February 14, 1908, in Jonathan E. Cox Papers.

25. "When J. Elwood Cox."

26. Cheney, *North Carolina Government*, 1395; Farriss, *High Point, North Carolina*, 94–95.

27. Connor and Poe, *Life and Speeches*, 276.

28. Connor and Poe, *Life and Speeches*, 95.

29. "Plants Consolidate."

30. "Tomlinson."

31. N.C. Department of Labor Statistics, *Eleventh Annual Report*, 63–64; N.C. Department of Labor and Printing, *Thirty-Second Report*, 64–68.

32. Pogacar, "White Family."

33. Jessup, "American Arts."

34. *North Carolina Year Book* (1916), 205–6.

35. U.S. Census Bureau, *Fourteenth Census of the United States*, 22–24.

36. Glass, *Textile Industry in North Carolina*, 57.

37. N.C. Department of Labor and Printing, *Thirty-Second Report*, 68.

38. N.C. Bureau of Labor and Printing, *Sixteenth Annual Report*, 192.

39. Lewis, "North Carolina Railroads."

40. N.C. Bureau of Labor and Printing, *Sixteenth Annual Report*, 141–45.

41. Drexel Enterprises, *Sixty Years*, 12.

42. Drexel Enterprises, *Sixty Years*, 20.

43. Drexel Enterprises, *Sixty Years*, 22–23.

44. *Pocket Directory*, 59.

45. *North Carolina Year Book* (1916), 274.

46. *North Carolina Year Book* (1922), 100, 105; Sanborn Map Company, "Marion, McDowell County, North Carolina, August 1922," in North Carolina Maps.

47. U.S. Census Bureau, *Fourteenth Census of the United States*, 22–24.

48. Mohney and Gray, "Hickory Southwest."

49. "Another Furniture Factory."

50. Sanborn Map Company, "Hickory, Catawba Co., North Carolina, April 1902," in North Carolina Maps; *North Carolina Year Book* (1903), 152–53.

51. Hickory Chair, "Then & Now."

52. U.S. Census Bureau, *Thirteenth Census of the United States*, 676–82.

53. N.C. Department of Labor and Printing, *Thirty-Second Report*, 64–69.

54. Hill Directory Company, *Greensboro, N.C., City Directory*, 79–80.

55. Miller, *Winston-Salem, N.C., City Directory*, 697–98.

56. "Our Furniture Industry."

57. Hall, Leloudis, Korstad, Murphy, Jones, and Daly, *Like a Family*, 174, 175.

58. Bamberger and Davidson, *Closing*, 25.

59. N.C. Department of Labor and Printing, *Thirty-Second Report*, 64–69.

60. Farriss, *High Point, North Carolina*, 9.

61. "High Point, North Carolina—Housing. Row of hovels occupied by colored workers from furniture and cotton mills," Lewis Hines Photographs for the National Research Project, 1936–37, National Archives.

62. U.S. Census Bureau, *Fifteenth Census of the United States: Population, Occupations*, 502.

63. "Boys 'linking' bed-springs. 14 and 15 years old," 1917, in National Child Labor Committee Collection; "World Furniture Company noon hour, Evansville, Inc. Boy at left hand end was running Machine Composed of two Unguarded Circular Saws. The board he was pushing stuck and he gave it an impatient shove. Had he slipped, both hands and arms would have gone into the edges of the saws, (full force) which were turned toward him," 1904, in National Child Labor Committee Collection.

64. E. Leroy Briggs, interview, February 7, 2008, in American Furniture Hall of Fame Oral Histories.

65. J. Wade Kincaid, interview by Robert A. Spelman, December 16, 1988, in American Furniture Hall of Fame Oral Histories.

66. N.C. Bureau of Labor and Printing, *Sixteenth Annual Report*, 155–56.

67. Bandow, "John Roberts."

68. U.S. Census Bureau, *Fourteenth Census of the United States*, 123. Traditionally, most jobs for women and girls in factories were in sewing and upholstery.

69. U.S. Census Bureau, *Fifteenth Census of the United States: Population, Occupations*, 1211.

70. "Marked Progress."

71. "Bankruptcy Sale!"; "Notice"; "The Bankrupt Sale."

72. "Hold a Stiff Upper Lip"; "Fuel Conservation."

73. "Business Slow."; "Furniture Industry." Stevens argues that Charles F. Tomlinson led the industry through the war years and was the force behind the beginning of its recovery in the early 1920s (*Anvil of Adversity*, 122).

74. Farriss, *High Point, North Carolina*, 28–29.

75. "High Point."

76. "Tomlinson of High Point."

77. "Do Laws of Conspiracy."

78. Selby, "Industrial Growth," 25–33.

79. "Mr. Cox Again"; "Editorial Notes"; "A Waiting Game."

80. Martinez, "Grand Rapids Furniture Strike of 1911."

81. *High Point, North Carolina, City Directory*.

82. "Labor Dispute."

83. "High Point Unionists"; "Unionists Picket."

84. "Business."

85. "The Contract."

86. "Picketing Grows."

87. Stevens, *Anvil of Adversity*, 45.

88. Stevens, *Anvil of Adversity*, 45.

89. "Furniture Makers."

90. McPherson, *High Pointers*, 22; "James T. Ryan."

91. Stevens, *Anvil of Adversity*, 53.

92. "Freight Rate Discrimination"; Jones, *Public Letters*, 18, 101.

93. "Changing the World"; Keller, "How a Small Southern Town."

94. McPherson, *High Pointers*, 22.

95. Stoesen, *Guilford County*, 24–25.

96. "Magnificent Display."

97. "Midsummer Furniture Show."

98. High Point Chamber of Commerce, "All about High Point," probably 1925, in High Point Museum Collection; High Point Chamber of Commerce, *High Point, North Carolina*, 6.

99. Emporis, "International Home Furnishings Center." Compared with Rose's other well-known work, such as the Goldsboro City Hall and the Cumberland County Courthouse, the exposition building's outer appearance is mostly utilitarian (Bushong, "Rose"). Its sides are plain, and there are no statues or ornate arches. The only decorations are the columns on the first two levels and two bands of neoclassical friezes (Bishir and Southern, *Guide*, 642–43).

100. U.S. Bureau of the Census, *Fourteenth Census of the United States*, 138.

CHAPTER 4. THE FURNITURE MARKET AND THE GOLDEN AGE

1. *Miller's High Point, N.C. City Directory*, 450–51.

2. Brown, "High Point."

3. N.C. Department of Labor, *Industrial Directory*, 82–93.

4. Hill Directory Company, *High Point City Directory*, 588–615.

5. "Sheraton Name."

6. "Guests Register."

7. "High Point's Magnificent New Hostelry."

8. Briggs, "High Point Skyscraper."

9. Binker, "Furniture Market History."

10. "Year 'round Exhibitors."

11. "Directory of Exhibitors."

12. "Markets"; N.C. Employment Security Commission, "Furniture," 5–6.

13. Inabinett, "Landmark."

14. *Miller's Thomasville, North Carolina, City Directory*, 221–37.

15. Phillips, "Thomasville Downtown Historic District."

16. N.C. Department of Labor, *Industrial Directory*; U.S. National Labor Relations Board, *Decisions and Orders*, 37:1019.

17. Doggett and Martin, *Lambert/Lambeth Family*, 468.

18. "Thomasville to Erect Big Chair."

19. "Thomasville Is Interested."

20. "Historical Landmark."

21. U.S. Census Bureau, *Fifteenth Census of the United States: Population, Number*, 784–804.

22. Stevens, *Anvil of Adversity*, 60–61.

23. Stevens, *Anvil of Adversity*, 65.

24. U.S. Census Bureau, *Fifteenth Census of the United States: Population, Number*, 784–804.

25. *Miller's Lenoir, North Carolina, City Directory*, 206–7.

26. Stevens, *Anvil of Adversity*, 21–28, 72.

27. Stevens, *Anvil of Adversity*, 90.

28. Stevens, *Anvil of Adversity*, 85–90.

29. Stevens, *Anvil of Adversity*, 106.

30. Stevens, *Anvil of Adversity*, 108–9.

31. "Respecting Distress"; Stevens, *Anvil of Adversity*, 109–10.

32. Macy, *Factory Man*, 62–64.

33. Macy, *Factory Man*, 89–90, 128–29, 132.

34. "Southern States."

35. Cater, "Rise of the Furniture Manufacturing Industry," 906–24.

36. Macy, *Factory Man*, 116.

37. Macy, *Factory Man*, 63.

38. Oliver, *Development and Structure*, 94.

39. "United Furniture."

40. U.S. Census Bureau, *Fifteenth Census of the United States: Manufactures*, 505.

41. Cater, "Rise of the Furniture Manufacturing Industry," 916–17.

42. U.S. Census Bureau, *Fifteenth Census of the United States: Manufactures*, 505.

43. N.C. Department of Environment and Natural Resources, "Catawba River Chain of Lakes," A413.

44. U.S. Census Bureau, *Fifteenth Census of the United States: Manufactures*, 511.

45. Oliver, *Development and Structure*, 136.

46. N.C. Employment Security Commission, *Occupational Information*, 21–29.

47. Haake, "Successful Dealer."

48. Wood, "Modern Furniture"; Ely, "Colors"; Butt, "Finest Decorative Furniture."

49. Drexel Enterprises, *Sixty Years*, 34.

50. "Tomlinson of High Point."

51. "The Braxton Chair," in Tomlinson of High Point, *Furniture by Tomlinson*.

52. "The Versailles Table Desk" and "The Carnac Arm Chair," in Tomlinson of High Point, *Furniture by Tomlinson*.

53. Korstian, *Economic Development of the Furniture Industry*, 15.

54. Korstian, *Economic Development of the Furniture Industry*, 16.

55. Korstian, *Economic Development of the Furniture Industry*, 10; N.C. Department of Labor, *Biennial Report, July 1, 1948 to June 30, 1950*, 96; N.C. Department of Labor, *Biennial Report, July 1, 1938 to June 30, 1940*, 61.

56. Selby, "'Better to Starve,'" 47.

57. U.S. Labor Department, *Wages and Hours of Labor in the Furniture Industry*; U.S. Labor Department, *Wages and Hours of Labor in Cotton-Goods Manufacturing*.

58. Glass, *Textile Industry in North Carolina*, 60.

59. U.S. National Labor Relations Board, *Decisions and Orders*, 55:1288.

60. *Miller's High Point, N.C. City Directory; Miller's Thomasville, North Carolina, City Directory*.

61. Yokely, "Current Cycle."

62. McCullough, "Was Warren C. Coleman."

63. Silva, "African American Millhands," 67–68.

64. Van Deusen, *Black Man in White America*, 116.

65. Gai and Minniti, "External Financing," 387–410; Weems and Randolph, "National Response," 75–76.

66. American Home Furnishings Hall of Fame, "Myrtle Hayworth Barthmaier"; "Wood Furniture."

67. David R. Hayworth, interview by Dorothy Gay Darr, February 6, 1997, in Southern Oral History Program Collection.

68. "Katherine Lambeth."

69. "Furniture Markets."

70. Hamilton, "'Sickness.'"

71. Hamilton, "'Sickness.'"

72. Selby, "'Better to Starve,'" 48.

73. "Tomlinson Chair Manufacturing Company Profit and Loss Statement for the Year Ended December 31, 1928," in Tomlinson of High Point, Inc. Records.

74. "Tomlinson Chair Manufacturing Company Exhibit B: Income and Profit and Loss Statement for the Six Months Ended June 30, 1932," in Tomlinson of High Point, Inc. Records.

75. "Financial Condition," in Tomlinson of High Point, Inc. Records.

76. Douty, "Labor Unrest," 581, 584.

77. Hall, Leloudis, Korstad, Murphy, Jones, and Daly, *Like a Family*, 328–32.

78. "400 Cotton Mill Workers."

79. Glass, *Textile Industry in North Carolina*, 69, 72; "Strike Situation"; "Tar Heel Liberals."

80. Selby, "'Better to Starve,'" 55.

81. Hall, Leloudis, Korstad, Murphy, Jones, and Daly, *Like a Family*, 290–92; Lefler and Newsome, *North Carolina*, 2:781–82.

82. "WPA Furniture"; "Furniture"; "Protest."

83. "Protest."

84. "Carolinians."

85. "Protest."

86. "A Message from Bus Hiatt, November 3, 1946," in M. H. Ross Papers.

87. U.S. National Labor Relations Board, Decisions and Orders, 37:1017–23.

88. Documents related to union elections in Tomlinson Furniture Company Mill #10, 1946, "Jurisdictional Dispute," in High Point Museum Collections.

89. Board of Governors of the Federal Reserve System, *Bank Suspensions*, 12.

90. "Business Briefs."

91. "Tobacco."

92. "Outlook"; "Business Briefs."

93. "Volume $25,000,000."

94. "Conversion."

95. "Furniture Factories."

96. Stevens, *Anvil of Adversity*, 122.

97. Stevens, *Anvil of Adversity*, 120–22.

98. "Kiwanis."

99. High Point Furniture and Woodworking Manufacturers' Association, *Woodworking*, 3.

100. High Point Furniture and Woodworking Manufacturers' Association, *Woodworking*, 4.

101. High Point Furniture and Woodworking Manufacturers' Association, *Woodworking*, 5.

102. High Point Furniture and Woodworking Manufacturers' Association, *Woodworking*, 8.

CHAPTER 5. PRESSURE AND COMPETITION

1. "Plan B Scratched"; Mooney, "Kennedy Flies."

2. "Small Crowd Cheers."

3. "Johnson Climbs Big Chair."

4. Jackson, *Crabgrass Frontier*, 232–33; Patterson, *Grand Expectations*, 78–80.

5. Hawkins, "A Corner View."

6. "Magnavox Factory."

7. Oliver, *Development and Structure*, 120–21.

8. Wainwright, "Shiny, Happy Households."

9. Cruse, "The Future."

10. "Furniture Fashions," 52, 53, 55, 59.

11. "Moore's."

12. "Burlington Industries," October 1982, in Burlington Industries, Inc., Records.

13. Douglas Brackett, interview by Tony Bengel, October 22, 2009, in American Furniture Hall of Fame Oral Histories.

14. Styers, "Good Afternoon."

15. O. William Fenn, Jr., interview by Tony Bengel, April 24, 2008, in American Furniture Hall of Fame Oral Histories.

16. Douglas Brackett, interview by Tony Bengel, October 22, 2009, in American Furniture Hall of Fame Oral Histories.

17. Drexel Enterprises, *Sixty Years*, 88.

18. Drexel Enterprises, *Sixty Years*, 69, 70–72.

19. "Armstrong Cork."

20. N.C. Department of Transportation, *Official Highway Map*, 1980, in North Carolina Maps.

21. N.C. Department of Labor, *North Carolina Directory*.

22. James Purdy to Douglas Brackett, March 17, 1975, and "North Carolina Air Quality Data," 1974, in American Furniture Manufacturers Association Records.

23. "Broyhill Furniture Industries," in Kepos, *International Directory*, 184–85.

24. "Wood Salutes."

25. Stevens, *Anvil of Adversity*, 111.

26. Stevens, *Anvil of Adversity*, 113.

27. Stevens, *Anvil of Adversity*, 120–23.

28. Stevens, *Anvil of Adversity*, 128–30.

29. Stevens, *Anvil of Adversity*, 197.

30. Stevens, *Anvil of Adversity*, 164–65.

31. Stevens, *Anvil of Adversity*, 115.

32. N.C. Department of Labor, *North Carolina Directory*.

33. Paul Hunt Broyhill, interview by Tony Bengel, October 28, 2010, in American Furniture Hall of Fame Oral Histories.

34. N.C. Department of Labor, *North Carolina Directory*.

35. Campbell, "4 Family Furniture Businesses"; Whitcomb, "Hickory Springs."

36. Rowland, "Furniture Manufacturers."

37. Hickory Furniture Mart, "Our History."

38. "Hickory Market."

39. Marks, "Finest Market."

40. "Furniture Highway."

41. N.C. Department of Labor, *North Carolina Directory*.

42. N.C. Department of Labor, *North Carolina Directory*.

43. N.C. Department of Labor, *North Carolina Directory*.

44. "White's Furniture."

45. Marks, "Furniture Mart."

46. N.C. Department of Labor, *North Carolina Directory*.

47. Marks, "Rites Held."

48. "Registration of Buyers, Southern Furniture Exposition Building, High Point, N.C., the Southern Market, April 19 to April 26, 1963," 50–76, in North Carolina Collection.

49. "Registration of Buyers, Southern Furniture Exposition Building, High Point, N.C., the Southern Market, April 19 to April 26, 1963," 41–49, 102–13, in North Carolina Collection.

50. "Registration of Buyers, Southern Furniture Exposition Building, High Point, N.C., the Southern Market, April 19 to April 26, 1963," 1–2, in North Carolina Collection.

51. McPherson, "Challenge."

52. Hawkings, "Fall Furniture."

53. N.C. Department of Labor, *North Carolina Directory*.

54. Knuemann, "Fun Furniture."

55. Duka, "Southern Furniture."

56. Marks, "High Point."

57. North Carolina State College and University of North Carolina, *Executive and Professional Education.*

58. North Carolina State College and University of North Carolina, *Executive and Professional Education.*

59. North Carolina State College and University of North Carolina, *Executive and Professional Education.*

60. "Professor"; Graham and Parrish, *Economic Possibilities*, 33; "Wrecked Plane."

61. "Announcements"; "Undergraduate Catalog."

62. C. Hubert Thomas to Dr. H. Edwin Beam, July 26, 1966, *Training for Industry*, in North Carolina Collection Photographic Archives.

63. Randolph Technical Institute, *Randolph Technical Institute General Catalog*, 89.

64. N.C. Department of Labor, *Biennial Report, July 1, 1950 to June 30, 1952*, 103.

65. Leifermann, "Trouble."

66. "Minimum Wage."

67. N.C. Department of Labor, *Biennial Report, July 1, 1970 to June 30, 1972*, 79.

68. Companies that produced upholstered furniture were even more averse to change than in the case goods field. William Fulmer notes that according to one furniture executive, the last major technological update in the field was that of the staple gun (*Negro in the Furniture Industry*, 76).

69. Fulmer, *Negro in the Furniture Industry*, 76.

70. Plice, *Manpower and Merger*, 13.

71. Plice, *Manpower and Merger*, 11.

72. "Kay Mfg."; "Vote for Union."

73. Bamberger and Davidson, *Closing*, 35.

74. "Union"; "Employees"; "Union Loses."

75. Fulmer, *Negro in the Furniture Industry*, 132.

76. Fulmer, *Negro in the Furniture Industry*, 25.

77. Fulmer, *Negro in the Furniture Industry*, 133–35.

78. Fulmer, *Negro in the Furniture Industry*, 67, 23.

79. Fulmer, *Negro in the Furniture Industry*, 102.

80. Fulmer, *Negro in the Furniture Industry*, 100.

81. "Myrtle Desk "; "U.S. Furniture Industries"; "A Better Community."

82. Fulmer, *Negro in the Furniture Industry*, 70.

83. *Role of the Small Businessman*, 68–75.

84. *Role of the Small Businessman*, 45, 45–50.

85. "Scott."

86. Nemeh, *Who's Who*, 282, 498, 1266.

87. Wrong, *Negro in the Apparel Industry*, 71.

88. John Christian Bernhardt, interview by Roy L. Briggs, July 15, 1992, and September 3, 1993, in American Furniture Hall of Fame Oral Histories.

89. Leisenring, "Equal Pay Day."

90. Patten, "Racial, Gender Wage Gaps."

91. N.C. Department of Natural and Economic Resources, *North Carolina*, 1.

92. "TFI"; Klemesrud, "At the Furniture Show"; Ibata, "Old Furniture Mart."

93. "All Work."

94. "Crider Building"; "Bowling"; "Champions."

95. "Howard."

96. Mulcahy, "A Beautiful Park"; "T. H. Broyhill Walking Park."

97. American Home Furnishings Hall of Fame, "George Alexander Bernhardt."

98. Duka, "Southern Furniture."

99. McPherson, "Good Afternoon."

100. McPherson, "Good Afternoon."

101. "Dolly Parton"; "Crowd Gives Standing Ovation"; "Things to Do."

102. U.S. Economic Analysis Bureau, "Full-Time and Part-Time Employees."

103. U.S. Department of Labor, *Employment*, 619–20.

CHAPTER 6. CHALLENGES AND RESILIENCE

1. Butler, "Historical S&P 500 Returns."

2. Boul, "High Point, N.C."

3. Vogel, "Home Design."

4. Nwagbara, Buehlmann, and Schuler, *Impact of Globalization*, 19–26.

5. U.S. Labor Statistics Bureau, "All Employees."

6. Trincia, "Furniture Sales Slump"; Cox, "Textile Industry Improves Profits."

7. Goldsmith, "Respiratory Disease"; Douglas Brackett, interview by Tony Bengel, October 22, 2009, in American Furniture Hall of Fame Oral Histories.

8. Douglass Brackett, interview by Tony Bengel, October 22, 2009, in American Furniture Hall of Fame Oral Histories.

9. Toner, "Incumbency."

10. Clendinen, "After Suicide."

11. Dionne, "Democrats Rejoice; Molotsky and Weaver, "Sanford's Seniority"; Cheney, *North Carolina Manual*, 1271.

12. Trincia, "Furniture Sales Slump."

13. Bamberger and Davidson, *Closing*, 30; Stevens, *Anvil of Adversity*, 107.

14. Daley, "The 'Giant Sucking Sound' of NAFTA."

15. U.S. Department of Justice, "Crime in the United States"; Federal Bureau of Investigation, "FBI Releases."

16. Nowell, "A Painful Goodbye"; Krishnan and Bonner, "A Fading Future"; Christianson, "Former Henredon Furniture Plant."

17. Nwagbara, Buehlmann, and Schuler, *Impact of Globalization*, 16.

18. U.S. Labor Statistics Bureau, "All Employees."

19. Hall, Leloudis, Korstad, Murphy, Jones, and Daly, *Like a Family*, 116; Firestone, "Chief Exporter."

20. U.S. Labor Statistics Bureau, "State and Area Employment."

21. Lacy, "Whither"; Mullin, "Rise and Sudden Decline."

22. Mullin, "Rise and Sudden Decline"; Conway, Connolly, Field, and Longman, "North Carolina Textiles Project."

23. Bamberger and Davidson, *Closing*, 126.

24. Bamberger and Davidson, *Closing*, 135.

25. Neal, "When the Last Factory."

26. Bamberger and Davidson, *Closing*, 122.

27. Bamberger and Davidson, *Closing*, 126–33.

28. Fox, Hargrove, and Bryden, "Economic Impact," 37–41.

29. Seymour, "Cozy."

30. Becker, "The Scene."

31. Becker, "The Scene."

32. Becker, "The Scene."

33. Schultz, "Polished-Up Market"; Bollinger, "High Point Market."

34. Binker, "Furniture Market History."

35. Karla Jones, interview by author, Bienenstock Furniture Library, High Point, N.C., April 1, 2022.

36. Schlichtman, "Temp Town," 5.

37. Schlichtman, "Temp Town," vi.

38. Schlichtman, "Temp Town," 194, 200–201.

39. "Yancey County"; Neal, "When the Last Factory."

40. Macy, *Factory Man*, 279, 281, 300, 374.

41. Sasso, "Lost Factory Jobs."

42. Mullin, "Rise and Sudden Decline"; Jones, "Ups and Downs."

43. Search results for the keyword "furniture factor" on the website Manufactured in North Carolina, maintained by North Carolina State University Industry Expansion Solutions and the North Carolina Manufacturing Extension Partnership (https://www.manufacturednc.com/search?keywords=furniture%20factory, accessed January 13, 2022).

44. Legg, "Maximising the Potential of CNC Routing Technology."

45. Tom Burke interview by Eric Medlin, July 23, 2021, Tomlinson/Erwin-Lambeth plant, Thomasville, North Carolina.

46. Levine, "North Carolina Discounters Offer Furniture Bargains."

47. Forsyth, "Retail Case Studies."

48. Richard Barentine, interview by Joseph Mosnier and Dorothy Gay Darr, January 28, 1999, in Southern Oral History Program Collection; Lail and Eller, *Hickory Furniture Mart*, 46.

49. Lail and Eller, *Hickory Furniture Mart*, 122.

50. Foster, "When Pandemic Reality Hits."

51. Bringle, "Design Lover's Guide."

52. Fox, Hargrove, and Bryden, "Economic Impact," 46.

53. Gregg, "Our Story."

54. David Williams, interview by author, March 11, 2022.

55. North Carolina State University, *Undergraduate Catalog 2017–2018*; North Carolina State University, "Physical Testing Lab."

56. University of North Carolina, Greensboro, *One-Hundred-and-Twenty-Eighth Annual University Catalog*; Appalachian State University, *2018–2019 Graduate Bulletin*; Western Carolina University, *Current 2021–2022 Undergraduate Catalog*.

57. Frick, "CVCC."

58. Caldwell Community College and Technical Institute, "History."

59. Bennington, *High Point University*, 58.

60. High Point University, *Undergraduate Bulletin*.

61. High Point University, "High Point University Students."

62. Fink, *Maya of Morganton*, 53.

63. Gill, *Latino Migration Experience*, 74, 87.

64. Coppedge, "A Culture Emerging."

65. J. Clyde Hooker Jr., interview by Roy Briggs, May 4, 1999, in American Furniture Hall of Fame Oral Histories.

66. Abrams, "A Second Chance."

67. Elkins, "Another Amazon Site."

68. Bollinger, "EGGER."

69. Hodgin, "10 Things."

EPILOGUE

1. Craver, "High Point Market Authority."

2. Savas, "High Point Market."

3. Smart, "Guests from 100+ Countries."

4. Smialek, "North Carolina's Furniture Hub."

5. Wear, "Coley Home"; Cooper, "Furniture Company."

6. Smialek, "North Carolina's Furniture Hub."

BIBLIOGRAPHY

ARCHIVAL COLLECTIONS

Most historical newspapers were found online at Newspapers.com from Ancestry and at *Chronicling America: Historic American Newspapers* (https://chroniclingamerica.loc.gov/) from the Library of Congress.

Alexander Crane Collection. Record ID PC.220. State Archives of North Carolina, Raleigh, N.C. https://axaem.archives.ncdcr.gov/findingaids/PC_220_Alexander_Crane_Collectio.html

American Furniture Hall of Fame Oral Histories, American Home Furnishings Hall of Fame, High Point, N.C.

American Furniture Manufacturers Association Records, 1905–94. Collection number 04957. Southern Historical Collection, University of North Carolina Libraries, Chapel Hill.

Burlington Industries, Inc. Records, 1844–2001. Collection number 04995. Southern Historical Collection, University of North Carolina Libraries, Chapel Hill.

High Point Museum, High Point, N.C.

Jonathan E. Cox Papers, 1885–1938, David M. Rubenstein Rare Book and Manuscript Library, Duke University, Durham, N.C. https://archives.lib.duke.edu/catalog/coxjonathane.

Lewis Hine Photographs for the National Research Project, 1936–37. Record Group 69, Records of the Work Projects Administration, 1922–44. National Archives, Washington, D.C.

M. H. Ross Papers, Southern Labor Archives, Special Collections and Archives, Georgia State University.

Museum of Early Southern Decorative Arts Collection, Winston-Salem, N.C.

National Child Labor Committee Collection, Prints and Photographs Division, Library of Congress.

North Carolina Collection, University of North Carolina Libraries, Chapel Hill.

North Carolina Collection Photographic Archives. University of North Carolina Libraries, Chapel Hill.

North Carolina Maps, University of North Carolina Libraries, Chapel Hill.

Southern Oral History Program Collection. Southern Historical Collection, University of North Carolina Libraries, Chapel Hill.

Tomlinson of High Point, Inc. Records, 1905–68. Collection number 04296. Southern Historical Collection, University of North Carolina Libraries, Chapel Hill.

SECONDARY SOURCES

Abrams, Amanda. "A Second Chance for North Carolina's Shuttered Factories." *New York Times*, June 15, 2021.

"All Work and No Play . . ." *Tomlinson News* (High Point, N.C.), January 1, 1952.

American Home Furnishings Hall of Fame. "George Alexander Bernhardt." https://www.homefurnishingshalloffame.com/george-alexander-bernhardt.

———. "Myrtle Hayworth Barthmaier." https://www.homefurnishingshalloffame .com/myrtle-haworth-barthmaier.

Andreas, A. T. *Cook County, Illinois: The Current Period to the Present Time*. Chicago: A. T. Andreas, 1884.

"Announcements for the Session 1955–1956." *State College Record* 54, no. 6 (1955).

"Another Furniture Factory." *Times-Mercury* (Hickory, N.C.), August 21, 1901.

Appalachian State University. *2018–2019 Graduate Bulletin*. http://bulletin .appstate.edu/content.php?catoid=10&navoid=518.

"Armstrong Cork Puts Okay on Two-for-One Stock Split." *High Point Enterprise*, January 29, 1969.

Bachynski, Kathleen, "American Medicine Was Built on the Backs of Slaves. And It Still Affects How Doctors Treat Patients Today." *Washington Post*, June 4, 2018.

Bamberger, Bill, and Cathy N. Davidson. *Closing: The Life and Death of an American Factory*. New Haven, Conn.: Yale University Art Gallery, 2001.

Bandow, Doug. "John Roberts: Rarely Has Such a Smart Judge Written Such a Bad Opinion." *Forbes*, July 2, 2012.

"Bankruptcy Sale!" *High Point Enterprise*, August 26, 1913.

"The Bankrupt Sale." *Concord (N.C.) Daily Tribune*, February 28, 1916.

Barrett, John Gilchrist. *The Civil War in North Carolina*. Chapel Hill: University of North Carolina Press, 1963.

Becker, Denise. "The Scene: Furniture Market—The Players: A Cast of 75,000, Including Buyers, Celebrities, Crashers." *Greensboro News and Record*, October 11, 2004.

Bennington, Richard R. *High Point University and the Furniture Industry*. Charleston, S.C.: History Press, 2021.

Berlin, Ira. "A Benevolent and Brutal Paternalism," *New York Times*, January 31, 1988.

"A Better Community. . ." *Winston-Salem Chronicle*, February 10, 1979.

Binker, Mark. "Furniture Market History." *Greensboro News and Record*, April 14, 2001.

Bishir, Catherine W., and Michael T. Southern. *A Guide to the Historic Architecture of Piedmont North Carolina*. Chapel Hill: University of North Carolina Press, 2003.

Bishop Furniture Company. Catalog. Grand Rapids, Mo., [1901?]. https://archive
.org/details/catalogoobish/mode/2up.

Bivins, John, Jr. *The Furniture of Coastal North Carolina, 1700–1820*. Winston-
Salem, N.C.: Museum of Early Southern Decorative Arts, 1988.

Board of Governors of the Federal Reserve System. *Bank Suspensions, 1892–1935*,
September 26, 1936. https://fraser.stlouisfed.org/title/bank-suspensions
-1892-1935-403.

Bollinger, Luke. "EGGER and Davidson County Community College Partner to
Help Fill 400 Jobs." *Triad Business Journal* (Greensboro, N.C.), May 1, 2018.

———. "High Point Market Brings Annual Impact of $6.73b, Report Finds." *Triad
Business Journal* (Greensboro, N.C.), February 14, 2019.

Bond, Lewis. "Cabinet-Making." *North Carolina Free Press* (Halifax), March 24,
1827.

"Bowling." *Statesville (N.C.) Record and Landmark*, October 10, 1972.

Boul, David. "High Point, N.C.: More Space for Furniture," *New York Times*, July
26, 1987.

*Branson's North Carolina Business Directory, for 1869, Containing Facts, Figures,
Names and Locations. Revised and Corrected Annually*. Raleigh: J. A. Jones
[1868]. https://archive.org/details/bransonsnorthcar1869rale/page/n63
/mode/2up.

Briggs, Benjamin. "High Point Skyscraper Recognized for History." *Preservation
Greensboro* (blog), October 22, 2009. https://preservationgreensboro.org
/high-point-skyscraper-recognized-for-history.

Bringle, Jennifer. "A Design Lover's Guide to High Point, the 'Furniture Capital
of the World.'" *Cardinal and Pine* (Durham, N.C.), August 9, 2021. https://
cardinalpine.com/story/a-design-lovers-guide-to-high-point-the-furniture
-capital-of-the-world.

Brown, Joe Exum. "High Point (and Nearby) Furniture Companies." July 17,
2001, revised and updated July 2003. https://www.highpointnc.gov
/DocumentCenter/View/1624/Furniture-List-File-PDF.

Bushong, William B. "Rose, William P. (1870–1952)," *North Carolina Architects and
Builders: A Biographical Dictionary*. Raleigh: Copyright and Digital Scholarship
Center, North Carolina State University Libraries, 2009.

"Business Briefs." *Daily Times-News* (Burlington, N.C.), April 10, 1935.

"Business Slow in Many Places." *Dispatch* (Lexington, N.C.), October 19, 1920.

"Business Soon Will Return to Normal in City." *High Point Enterprise*, extra, September 14, 1919.

Butler, Dave. "Historical S&P 500 Returns." *The Street* (New York), May 5, 2020.
https://www.thestreet.com/investing/annual-sp-500-returns-in-history.

Butt, G. Baseden. "Finest Decorative Furniture Is Veneered." *Furniture South*, May 1927, 99.

Byrne, William A. "The Hiring of Woodson, Slave Carpenter of Savannah." *Georgia Historical Quarterly* 77, no. 2 (1993): 245–63.

Caldwell Community College and Technical Institute. "History of the College." http://cccti.smartcatalogiq.com/2020-2021/College-Catalog /General-Information/History-of-the-College.

Campbell, Courtney. "4 Family Furniture Businesses Built to Last." *Our State* (Greensboro, N.C.), May 10, 2017.

"Carolinians Winners in Furniture Plant Battle." *Lenoir (N.C.) News-Topic*, March 8, 1934.

Carron, Christian G. *Grand Rapids Furniture: The Story of America's Furniture City*. Grand Rapids, Mich.: Public Museum of Grand Rapids, 1998.

Cater, John James. "The Rise of the Furniture Manufacturing Industry in Western North Carolina and Virginia." *Management Decision* 43, no. 6 (2005): 906–24.

"Champions for Third Straight Year." *High Point Enterprise*, August 8, 1974.

"Changing the World One Desk at a Time: 110 Years of High Point Furniture Market." *High Point Discovered*, March 22, 2019. https://highpointdiscovered.org /magazine/130-years-of-high-point-furniture-market.

Cheney, John L. *North Carolina Government, 1585–1974: A Narrative and Statistical History*. Raleigh: N.C. Department of the Secretary of State, 1975.

———, ed. *North Carolina Manual, 1987–1988*. Raleigh: State of North Carolina, 1987.

Christianson, Rich. "Former Henredon Furniture Plant Bull-Dozed for Walmart Store." *Woodworking Network*, July 24, 2012. https://www .woodworkingnetwork.com/wood-market-trends/woodworking -industry-news/production-woodworking-news/Fomrer-Henredon-Furniture -Plant-to-Become-a-Walmart-Store-163546306.html.

City of Winston-Salem. "Town of Salem: 1763–1792." https://www.cityofws.org /DocumentCenter/View/2817/Salem-1763-to-1792-PDF.

Clayton, Ralph. "E. A. Poe, Dealer in Slaves." *Baltimore Sun*, October 1, 1993.

Clendinen, Dudley. "After Suicide, Speculation Focuses on Broyhill for Senate Seat." *New York Times*, July 1, 1986.

Connor, R. D. W., and Clarence Poe. *The Life and Speeches of Charles Brantley Aycock*. Garden City, New York: Doubleday Page, 1912.

"The Contract." *High Point Enterprise*, extra, September 14, 1919.

"Conversion of Wood Furniture Industry Is Now Being Sought." *High Point Enterprise*, April 27, 1942.

Conway, Patrick, Robert Connolly, Alfred Field, and Douglas Longman. "The North Carolina Textiles Project: An Initial Report." University of North Carolina, Chapel Hill, November 7, 2003. https://pconway.web.unc.edu /wp-content/uploads/sites/11310/2015/12/nctp_tatm_rev.pdf.

Cooper, John Milton. *Walter Hines Page: The Southerner as American, 1855–1918.* Chapel Hill: University of North Carolina Press, 1977.

Cooper, Roy. "Furniture Company to Add New Production Facility and 90 New Jobs in Catawba County." N.C. Governor's Office news release, December 3, 2021. https://governor.nc.gov/news/press-releases/2021/12/03 /furniture-company-add-new-production-facility-and-90-new-jobs -catawba-county.

Coppedge, Michelle. "A Culture Emerging." *Endeavors* (blog), University of North Carolina, May 1, 2004. https://endeavors.unc.edu/spr2004/latino.html.

Cox, Staci. "Textile Industry Improves Profits." *Daily Tar Heel* (Chapel Hill, N.C.), January 27, 1988.

Craver, Richard. "High Point Market Authority Cancels Spring Trade Show; First Time since World War II." *Greensboro News and Record*, April 16, 2020. https:// greensboro.com/news/local_news/high-point-market-authority-cancels -spring-trade-show-first-time-since-world-war-ii/article_1115b087-fa26-5dc1 -827f-608dbfaefc80.html.

"Crider Building Falls to M&J." *Statesville (N.C.) Record and Landmark*, June 3, 1971.

"Crowd Gives Standing Ovation to Theater's First Performers." *High Point Enterprise*, October 8, 1975.

Cruse, William T. "The Future of Plastics in Furniture." *Furniture South*, February 1967.

Daley, Beth. "The 'Giant Sucking Sound' of NAFTA: Ross Perot Was Ridiculed as Alarmist in 1992 but His Warning Turned Out to Be Prescient." *Conversation U.S.* (Boston, MA). July 12, 2019. https://theconversation.com /the-giant-sucking-sound-of-nafta-ross-perot-was-ridiculed-as-alarmist -in-1992-but-his-warning-turned-out-to-be-prescient-120258.

Darr, Dorothy Gay, and M. Ruth Little. "West High Street Historic District, High Point, Guilford County." National Register of Historic Places Nomination. Raleigh: N.C. State Historic Preservation Office, 2007. https://files.nc.gov/ncdcr /nr/GF2986.pdf.

Dionne, E. J., Jr. "Democrats Rejoice at 55-45 Senate Margin but Still Seek Agenda to Counter Reagan; Big Political Shift." *New York Times*, November 6, 1986.

"Directory of Exhibitors." *Furniture South*, July 1929, 36–37.

Doggett, Mary Norton, and Sophie Stephens Martin. *The Lambert/Lambeth Family of North Carolina.* Greensboro, N.C.: Lambeth Family Connection, 1947. https://archive.org/details/lambertlambethfa000dogg.

"Do Laws of Conspiracy Cover Union Boycotts?" *Morning Post* (Raleigh, N.C.), November 1, 1904.

"Dolly Parton to Appear in Concert Here." *High Point Enterprise*, October 17, 1976.

Douty, H. M. "Labor Unrest in North Carolina, 1932." *Social Forces* 11, no. 4 (1933): 579–88.

Drexel Enterprises. *Sixty Years of Progress in the Making of Fine Furniture, 1903–1963.* Drexel, N.C.: Drexel Enterprises, 1963.

Duka, John. "The Southern Furniture Market: A Collision of Tastes." *New York Times*, April 20, 1978.

Ebert, Charles H. V. "High Point's Evolution as a Furniture Town." PhD diss., University of North Carolina at Chapel Hill, 1953.

"Editorial Notes." *Labor News* (Greensboro, N.C.), August 20, 1909.

Elkins, Ken. "Another Amazon Site Proposed; Can You Say HQ2 Hickory?" *Charlotte Business Journal*, October 9, 2017.

Ely, Edwin W. "Colors in Commerce." *Furniture South*, January 1929, 43.

"Employees Reject Union in Election at Henredon." *News Herald* (Morganton, N.C.), May 23, 1975.

Emporis. "International Home Furnishings Center." https://www.emporis.com /buildings/125214/international-home-furnishings-center-high-point-nc-usa.

Farriss, J. J. *High Point, N.C.: A Brief Summary of Its Manufacturing Enterprises, Together with Sketches of Those Who Have Built Them.* [High Point, N.C.?], 1896. https://archive.org/details/highpointnorthca1896farr/mode/2up.

——. *High Point, N.C.: A Brief Summary of Its Manufacturing Enterprises, Together with Sketches of Those Who Have Built Them.* [High Point, N.C.?], 1900. https:// archive.org/details/highpointnorthca1900farr/page/n11/mode/2up.

——. *High Point, North Carolina.* 7th ed. [High Point, N.C.?], [1915?].https:// archive.org/details/highpointnorthca1915farr/page/n55/mode/2up.

Fink, Leon. *The Maya of Morganton: Work and Community in the Nuevo South.* Chapel Hill: University of North Carolina Press, 2003.

Finkelman, Paul. "America's 'Great Chief Justice' Was an Unrepentant Slaveholder." *Atlantic*, June 15, 2021.

Firestone, David. "A Chief Exporter, and Not at All Pleased About It." *New York Times*, February 23, 2001.

Forsyth, Angela. "Retail Case Studies: Furnitureland South." *Retail and Hospitality Hub*, April 2, 2019, https://retailandhospitalityhub.com/retail /retail-case-studies/furnitureland-south.

Foster, R. Daniel. "When Pandemic Reality Hits Reality Real Estate Shows." *Los Angeles Times*, May 5, 2020.

"400 Cotton Mill Workers Strike at Thomasville." *Statesville (N.C.) Record and Landmark*, August 30, 1932.

Fox, Gerald T., Richard M. Hargrove, and David L. Bryden. *The Economic Impact of the Home Furnishings Industry in the Triad Region of North Carolina*. High Point: High Point University, May 2007. http://acme.highpoint.edu/~jfox /HPUStudy.pdf

Franklin, John Hope. *The Free Negro in North Carolina, 1790–1860*. Chapel Hill: University of North Carolina Press, 1943.

"Freight Rate Discrimination." *High Point Enterprise*, April 9, 1912.

Frick, Alex. "CVCC Unveils New Furniture Academy." *Hickory Daily Record*, October 7, 2014.

Fries, Adelaide L., ed. *Records of the Moravians in North Carolina*. Vol. 5, *1784–1792*. Raleigh: Historical Commission, 1941.

———. *Records of the Moravians in North Carolina*. Vol. 7, *1809–1822*. Raleigh: State Department of Archives and History, 1947.

Fries, Adelaide L., and Douglas LeTell Rights, eds. *Records of the Moravians in North Carolina*. Vol. 8, *1823–1837*. Raleigh: State Department of Archives and History, 1954.

"Fuel Conservation Close Local Factories." *High Point Enterprise*, January 17, 1918.

Fulmer, William E. *The Negro in the Furniture Industry*. The Racial Policies of American Industry, Report No. 28. Philadelphia: Industrial Research Unit, Wharton School, University of Pennsylvania, 1973.

"Furniture." *Wilmington Morning Star*, May 30, 1880.

"Furniture Factories May Be Used for Manufacture of Airplanes in 'All-Out' War Effort of Nation." *High Point Enterprise*, March 29, 1942.

"Furniture Fashions." *Furniture South*, January 1972.

"Furniture Highway Booms with Expanded Facilities." *High Point Enterprise*, October 20, 1963.

"Furniture Industry Still Lively." *Review* (High Point, N.C.), September 9, 1920.

"Furniture Makers." *Morning Post* (Raleigh, N.C.), November 21, 1901.

"The Furniture Markets and the Furniture Prospect." *Furniture South*, February 1929, 14.

"Furniture Men Make Protest." *Hickory Daily Record*, July 18, 1934.

Gai, Yunwei, and Maria Minniti. "External Financing and the Survival of Black-Owned Start-ups in the U.S." *Eastern Economic Journal* 41, no. 3 (2015): 387–410.

Genovese, Eugene D. *Roll, Jordan, Roll: The World the Slaves Made*. New York: Pantheon, 1974.

Gill, Hannah. *The Latino Migration Experience in North Carolina: New Roots in the Old North State*. Chapel Hill: University of North Carolina Press, 2010.

Glass, Brent D. *The Textile Industry in North Carolina: A History*. Raleigh: Division of Archives and History, N.C. Department of Cultural Resources, 1992.

"Goldsboro Gossip." *Wilmington Messenger*, September 22, 1900.

"Goldsboro's Growth." *State Chronicle* (Raleigh, N.C.), April 3, 1890.

Goldsmith, David F. "Respiratory Disease in the North Carolina Furniture Industry: A Pilot Study." PhD diss., University of North Carolina, Chapel Hill, 1983.

Graham, Paul H., and Frank T. Parrish. *The Economic Possibilities of Wood Particle Board Manufacture in Maine*. Washington, D.C.: Small Business Administration, June 1961.

Gregg, Carol. "Our Story." Red Egg, https://redegg.com/story.

"Guests Register at the Sheraton First Time Today." *High Point Enterprise*, October 29, 1921.

Haake, A. P. "The Successful Dealer Must Study Style and Design." *Furniture South*, January 1931, 17.

Hall, Jacquelyn Dowd, James L. Leloudis, Robert Rodgers Korstad, Mary Murphy, Lu Ann Jones, and Christopher B. Daly. *Like a Family: The Making of a Southern Cotton Mill World*. Chapel Hill: University of North Carolina Press, 2000.

Hamilton, C. B. "The 'Sickness' of the Furniture Business." *Furniture South*, July 1929, 13.

Harden, John. *Boling: The Story of a Company and Family*. Siler City, N.C.: Boling, 1980.

Hawkins, Jim. "A Corner View of Guilford." *High Point Enterprise*, October 27, 1967.

———. "Fall Furniture Market Opens." *High Point Enterprise*, October 23, 1975.

Hazzard, J. L. *A New Map of the State of North Carolina*. Philadelphia: Charles Desilver, 1860. https://dc.lib.unc.edu/cdm/singleitem/collection/ncmaps/id/83/rec/2

Hergesheimer, Edwin. *Map Showing the Distribution of the Slave Population of the Southern States of the United States. Compiled from the Census of 1860*. Washington, D.C.: Henry S. Graham. https://www.loc.gov/item/99447026.

Hickory Chair. "Then & Now: Milestones in Hickory Chair's Hundred-Year History." http://www.hickorychair.com/Misc/ThenNow.

Hickory Furniture Mart. "Our History." https://www.hickoryfurniture.com/about/history/.

"Hickory Market Announces Plan for Expansion." *High Point Enterprise*, April 22, 1976.

"High Point." *Labor News* (Greensboro, N.C.), September 17, 1909.

High Point Chamber of Commerce. *The Building and the Builders of a City: High Point, North Carolina.* High Point, N.C.: Hall Print, 1947. https://archive.org/details/buildingbuilders00comp/page/n3/mode/2up.

———. *High Point, North Carolina: The Industrial City of the South.* High Point, N.C.: High Point Chamber of Commerce, [1923?]. https://archive.org/details/highpointnorthca1923guil/mode/2up.

High Point Furniture Company. *Six Great Leaders from High Point Furniture Company, High Point, North Carolina.* [High Point, N.C.], 1901.

High Point Furniture and Woodworking Manufacturers' Association. *Woodworking for War: Men—Materials—Machines Mobilized in High Point, N.C.* High Point, N.C.: Hall Printing, [1942?]. https://archive.org/details/woodworkingforwa00high/mode/2up.

"High Point Is in It!" *Durham Daily Globe,* September 27, 1892.

High Point, North Carolina, City Directory. Vol. 5, *1919.* Columbia, S.C.: The State Company, 1918. https://archive.org/stream/highpointnccitydo5pied/highpointnccitydo5pied_djvu.txt.

"High Point's Magnificent New Hostelry Opens Today." *High Point Enterprise,* November 22, 1921.

"High Point Unionists Picketing Factories with Visible Effect." *Greensboro Daily News,* August 21, 1919.

High Point University. "High Point University Students Gain Hands-On Experience at High Point Furniture Market." News release, October 18, 2019. https://www.highpoint.edu/blog/2019/10/high-point-university-students-gain-hands-on-experience-at-high-point-furniture-market.

High Point University. *Undergraduate Bulletin, 2019–2020.* https://www.highpoint.edu/registrar/files/2019-2020-Undergraduate-Bulletin.pdf.

Hill Directory Company. *Greensboro, N.C., City Directory, 1922.* Richmond, Va.: Hill Directory, 1922. https://archive.org/details/greensboroguilfo1922unse/page/n3/mode/2up

———. *High Point City Directory, 1935.* n.p.: Hill Directory, 1935.

"Historical Landmark Seated in Thomasville." *Dispatch* (Lexington, N.C.), June 1, 2001.

"History Headlines," *OAH Magazine of History* 15, no. 2 (2001): 71–72.

Hodgin, Carrie. "10 Things You Might Not Know about Lexington's BBQ Past." *WFMY* (Greensboro, N.C.), October 22, 2018.

"Hold a Stiff Upper Lip." *Dispatch* (Lexington, N.C.), December 3, 1920.

"Howard a Two-Time Labor Day Winner." *Gastonia Gazette,* September 6, 1973.

Huber, Patrick. "Mill Mother's Lament: Ella May Wiggins and the Gastonia Textile Strike of 1929." *Southern Cultures* 15, no. 3 (2009): 81–110.

Huffman, Robert O. *Drexel Enterprises, Inc.: A Brief History*. New York: Newcomen Society in North America, 1963.

Ibata, David. "Old Furniture Mart Now within Chemical's Grasp." *Chicago Tribune*, April 13, 1987.

Idol, Vera. "High Pointer of the Week: A. W. Klemme." *High Point Enterprise*, May 22, 1960.

Inabinett, Marian. "A Landmark That Never Goes Out-of-Style." *History Hindsights from the High Point Museum* (blog), January 20, 2021. https://www .highpointnc.gov/Blog.aspx?IID=42#item.

Jackson, Kenneth T. *Crabgrass Frontier: The Suburbanization of the United States*. New York: Oxford University Press, 1985.

"James T. Ryan, Ex-Official of Furniture Group in South." *New York Times*, April 24, 1968.

Jessup, Lynn. "American Arts and Crafts Rejuvenated." *Greensville News and Record*, April 26, 1995.

"Johnson Climbs Big Chair during Stop in Thomasville." *High Point Enterprise*, October 11, 1960.

Jones, Mary Helen. "The Ups and Downs of the Furniture Capital." *Spectrum News* (Greensboro, N.C.), March 19, 2021. https://spectrumlocalnews.com/nc /triad/news/2021/03/19/the-ups-and-downs-of-the-furniture-capital.

Jones, May F., ed. *Public Letters and Papers of Locke Craig, Governor of North Carolina, 1913–1917*. Raleigh: Edwards and Broughton, 1916. https://archive.org /details/publiclett19131917nort/page/10/mode/2up?q=furniture

Journals of the Senate and House of Commons of the General Assembly of the State of North Carolina, at the Session of 1830–31. Raleigh: Lawrence and Lemay, 1831. https://archive.org/details/journalsofsenate18301831/mode/2up.

"Jurisdictional Dispute Ended in Thomasville." *High Point Enterprise*, June 25, 1942.

"Justice's Weekly Letter." *Union Republican* (Winston-Salem, N.C.), September 10, 1908.

"Katherine Lambeth." *Greensboro News and Record*, October 25, 1998.

"Kay Mfg Asks for Election." *High Point Enterprise*, January 14, 1960.

Keller, Hadley. "How a Small Southern Town Became the Furniture Capital of America." *Architectural Digest*, October 13, 2017.

Kepos, Paula, ed. *International Directory of Company Histories*. Vol. 10. Chicago: St. James, 1995.

Ketchum, William C. Jr., with the Museum of American Folk Art. *American Cabinetmakers: Marked American Furniture, 1640–1940*. New York: Crown, 1995.

"Kiwanis Receives Four New Members." *Statesville (N.C.) Record and Landmark,*
    June 21, 1943.

Klemesrud, Judy. "At the Furniture Show, There's Little New—Except the Mood."
    New York Times, January 11, 1974.

Korstad, Robert Rogers. *Civil Rights Unionism: Tobacco Workers and the Struggle
    for Democracy in the Mid-Twentieth-Century South.* Chapel Hill: University of
    North Carolina Press, 2003.

Korstian, Clarence F. *The Economic Development of the Furniture Industry of the
    South and Its Future Dependence upon Forestry.* Raleigh: N.C. Department of
    Conservation and Development, Division of Forestry, 1926.

Knuemann, Carolyn. "Fun Furniture Popular in American Homes." *Daily Times-
    News* (Burlington, N.C.), August 10, 1960.

Krishnan, Anne, and Paul Bonner. "A Fading Future: The Furniture Industry—A
    Pillar of the State's Economy—May Soon Be Gone." *Herald Sun* (Durham,
    N.C.), February 15, 2004.

"Labor Dispute at Hickory Chair Co." *Hickory Daily Record* (Hickory, N.C.), March
    22, 1918.

Lacy, Robert L. "Whither North Carolina Furniture Manufacturing?" Working
    Paper 04–07, Federal Reserve Bank of Richmond, September 2004. https://
    fraser.stlouisfed.org/title/3942/item/477141.

Lail, G. Leroy, and Richard Eller. *Hickory Furniture Mart: A Landmark History: 60
    Years of Market Development.* Hickory, N.C.: Redhawk, [2020?].

Larson, Mary. "Potential, Potential, Potential: The Marriage of Oral History and
    the World Wide Web," *Journal of American History* 88, no. 2 (2001): 596–603.

Lefler, Hugh Talmage, and Albert Ray Newsome. *North Carolina: The History of a
    Southern State.* Chapel Hill: University of North Carolina Press, 1954.

Legg, John. "Maximising the Potential of CNC Routing Technology." *Furniture
    and Joinery Production,* January 25, 2018. https://www.furnitureproduction
    .net/resources/articles/2018/01/1371460764-maximising-potential-cnc
    -routing-technology.

Leifermann, Henry P. "Trouble in the South's First Industry," *New York Times,*
    August 5, 1973.

Leisenring, Mary. "Equal Pay Day Is March 31—the Earliest since It Began in
    1996." *America Counts: Stories behind the Numbers* (blog), March 31, 2020.
    https://www.census.gov/library/stories/2020/03/equal-pay-day-is-march-31
    -earliest-since-1996.html.

Levine, Lisbeth. "North Carolina Discounters Offer Furniture Bargains." *New York
    Times,* April 17, 1986.

Lewis, J. D. "North Carolina Railroads—1910—Miscellaneous Railroads." Caro-

lana, 2018, https://www.carolana.com/NC/Transportation/railroads
/nc_railroads_1910_misc_rrs.htm.

Lowry, Dan Mabry. "The Beginnings of Industrialism in North Carolina, 1865–1900." PhD diss., University of North Carolina, Chapel Hill, 1935.

Macy, Beth. *Factory Man: How One Furniture Maker Battled Offshoring, Stayed Local—and Helped Save an American Town*. New York: Little, Brown, 2014.

"Magnavox Factory Showroom Samples." *High Point Enterprise*, November 7, 1975.

"Magnificent Display of Furniture throughout the City in the Various Exposition Rooms." *High Point Enterprise*, June 25, 1913.

Manufactures of the United States in 1860; Compiled from the Original Returns of the Eighth Census, under the Direction of the Secretary of the Interior. Washington, D.C.: Government Printing Office, 1865. https://www2.census.gov/library /publications/decennial/1860/manufactures.

"Marked Progress in Furniture Industry." *Greensboro Daily News*, July 23, 1915.

"Markets Followed Industry's Growth." *High Point Enterprise*, October 20, 1967.

Marks, Robert. "Finest Market Seen." *High Point Enterprise*, April 13, 1975.

———. "Furniture Mart Changes Started." *High Point Enterprise*, July 12, 1964.

———. "High Point to Open Furniture Library Thursday." *Gastonia Gazette*, April 5, 1970.

———. "Rites Held for New Exposition Annex." *High Point Enterprise*, October 18, 1965.

Marshall, Patricia Phillips, and Jo Ramsay Leimenstoll. *Thomas Day: Master Craftsman and Free Man of Color*. Chapel Hill: N.C. Museum of History and University of North Carolina Press, 2010.

Martinez, Shandra. "Grand Rapids Furniture Strike of 1911 Led to Wild Riot, Left Lessons in its Wake." *Michigan Live* (Grand Rapids, MI), April 3, 2019. https:// www.mlive.com/business/west-michigan/2011/04/grand_rapids_furniture _strike.html.

McCullough, Norman J., Sr. "Was Warren C. Coleman the Richest African-American in America in 1900?" *Independent Tribune* (Concord, N.C.), March 27, 2019.

McPherson, Holt. "Challenge Is on to Save Downtown." *High Point Enterprise*, June 29, 1975.

———. *High Pointers of High Point*. High Point, N.C.: Chamber of Commerce of High Point, 1976. https://archive.org/details/highpointersofhi01mcph /page/18/mode/2up.

Medearis, C. Alan. "The Furniture Industry and Its Retail Distribution." Honors essay, University of North Carolina, Chapel Hill, 1976.

"Messenger Bureau, Raleigh, December 5." *Semi-Weekly Messenger* (Wilmington, N.C.), December 11, 1900.

"The Midsummer Furniture Show Opens in High Point Next Monday." *High Point Enterprise*, July 11, 1914.

Miller, Ernest H. *Miller's High Point, N.C., City Directory*. Vol. 11, 1929–1930. Asheville, N.C.: Miller, 1929. https://archive.org/details/millershighpoint11mill/page/n5/mode/2up.

———. *Miller's Lenoir, North Carolina, City Directory*. Vol. 1, 1930–1931. Asheville: Commercial Service, 1930.

———. *Miller's Thomasville, North Carolina, City Directory*. Vol. 1, 1928–1929. Asheville: Commercial Service, 1928.

———. *Winston-Salem, N.C., City Directory*. Vol. 19, 1921. Fort Wayne, Ind.: Fort Wayne Box, Printers, [1921?]. https://archive.org/details/winstonsalemncci19pied/page/698/mode/2up.

"Minimum Wage Boost to Affect 170,000 in State." *Statesville (N.C.) Record and Landmark*, February 28, 1956.

Mohney, Kirk, and Stewart Gray. "Hickory Southwest Downtown Historic District, Hickory, Catawba County." National Register of Historic Places Nomination. Raleigh: N.C. State Historic Preservation Office, 2005. https://files.nc.gov/ncdcr/nr/CT1082.pdf.

Molotsky, Irvin, and Warren Weaver Jr. "Sanford's Seniority." *New York Times*, November 15, 1986.

Moonan, Wendy. "Antiques." *New York Times*, January 16, 2004.

Mooney, J. W. P. "Kennedy Flies into Local Airport." *High Point Enterprise*, September 17, 1960.

"Moore's." *Daily Times-News* (Burlington, N.C.), February 16, 1972.

"The Morganton Furniture Manufacturing Company." *Charlotte Democrat*, February 6, 1885.

"Mr. Cox Again." *Labor News* (Greensboro, N.C.), October 2, 1908.

"Mr. Cox Welcomed Home." *Union Republican* (Winston-Salem, N.C.), September 3, 1908.

Mulcahy, Chris. "A Beautiful Park to Put on Your North Carolina Bucket List." *WCNC* (Greensboro, N.C.), February 25, 2021.

Mullin, John. "The Rise and Sudden Decline of North Carolina Furniture Making." *Econ Focus*, 2020, 16–19. https://www.richmondfed.org/publications/research/econ_focus/2020/q4/economic_history.

"The Municipal Elections." *Asheville (N.C.) Weekly Citizen*, May 14, 1891.

"Museum Motifs." *Colonial Homes*, September/October 1986, 157.

"Myrtle Desk Needs Skilled Furniture Craftsmen and Interested Trainees." *Tribunal Aid* (High Point, N.C.), July 4, 1973.

Neal, Dale. "When the Last Factory Leaves a Mountain Town." *Citizen-Times* (Asheville, N.C.), August 30, 2014.

N.C. Bureau of Labor and Printing. *Eleventh Annual Report of the Bureau of Labor Statistics of North Carolina*. Raleigh: Guy V. Barnes, 1898.

———. *Fifth Annual Report of the Bureau of Labor Statistics for the State of North Carolina*. Raleigh: Josephus Daniels, 1892.

———. *Fourth Annual Report of the Bureau of Labor Statistics for the State of North Carolina*. Raleigh: Josephus Daniels, 1890.

———. *Ninth Annual Report of the Bureau of Labor Statistics of the State of North Carolina*. Winston: M. L. and J. C. Stewart, 1895.

———. *Sixteenth Annual Report of the Bureau of Labor and Printing of the State of North Carolina*. Raleigh: Edwards and Broughton, 1903.

———. *Twelfth Annual Report of the Bureau of Labor Statistics of North Carolina,*. Raleigh: Guy V. Barnes, 1899.

N.C. Department of Environment and Natural Resources, Division of Water Quality. "Catawba River Chain of Lakes." In *Catawba River Basinwide Water Quality Plan*. Raleigh: N.C. Department of Environment and Natural Resources, September 2010. https://files.nc.gov/ncdeq/Water%20Quality/Planning/BPU/BPU/Catawba/Catawba%20Plans/2010%20Plan/Chapter%204%20-%20Chain%20of%20Lakes.pdf

N.C. Department of Labor. *Biennial Report of the Department of Labor, July 1, 1938 to June 30, 1940*. Raleigh: N.C. Department of Labor, 1940.

———. *Biennial Report of the Department of Labor, July 1, 1948 to June 30, 1950*. Durham: Christian Printing, July 1950.

———. *Biennial Report of the Department of Labor, July 1, 1950 to June 30, 1952*. Durham: Christian Printing, 1952.

———. *Biennial Report of the Department of Labor, July 1, 1970 to June 30, 1972*. Raleigh: N.C. Department of Labor, 1972.

———. *Industrial Directory and Reference Book*. Durham: Christian Printing, 1938.

———. *North Carolina Directory of Manufacturing Firms, 1968*. Durham: Christian Printing, [1968?].

N.C. Department of Labor and Printing. *Thirty-Second Report of the Department of Labor and Printing of the State of North Carolina*. Raleigh: Edwards and Broughton, 1921.

N.C. Department of Natural and Economic Resources. *North Carolina, the Largest Furniture Producing State in the Nation*. Raleigh: Research and Statistics Section, 1972.

N.C. Employment Security Commission. "Furniture, Started Early, among State's Leading Industries." *ESC Quarterly* 10, nos. 1–2 (1952), 5–6.

———. *Occupational Information on Furniture Manufacturing in North Carolina*. Raleigh: N.C. Employment Security Commission, 1947.

N.C. General Assembly. *Laws and Resolutions of the State of North Carolina, Passed by the General Assembly at Its Session of 1879*. Raleigh: Observer 1879.

Nemeh, Katherine H., ed. *Who's Who among African Americans*. Detroit: Thomson Gale, 2005. North Carolina State College and University of North Carolina. *Executive and Professional Education for the Southern Furniture Industry in Industrial Engineering and Business Management*. Raleigh: State College of Agriculture and Engineering, 1946.

North Carolina State University. "Physical Testing Lab." Center for Additive Manufacturing and Logistics. https://www.camal.ncsu.edu/industry-partners -camal/services/physical-testing-lab.

———. *Undergraduate Catalog 2017–2018*. http://catalog.ncsu.edu/pdf/2017-2018 .pdf.

North Carolina Year Book, 1922. Raleigh: News and Observer, [1922?]. https:// archive.org/details/northcarolinayea1922rale/mode/2up.

North Carolina Year Book and Business Directory, 1903. Raleigh: News and Observer, [1903?]. https://archive.org/details/northcarolinayea1903rale /mode/2up.

North Carolina Year Book and Business Directory, 1904. Raleigh: News and Observer, [1904?]. https://archive.org/details/northcarolinayea1904rale /page/296/mode/2up.

North Carolina Year Book and Business Directory, 1916. Raleigh: News and Observer, [1916?]. https://archive.org/details/northcarolinayea1916rale/page/274 /mode/2up.

"Notice." *Everything* (Greensboro, N.C.), November 13, 1915.

"Notice of Incorporation." *Goldsboro Messenger*, May 23, 1887.

Nowell, Paul. "A Painful Goodbye: Factory Closing after Nearly a Century." *Greensboro News and Record*, January 16, 2002.

Nwagbara, Ucheoma, Urs Buehlmann, and Al Schuler, *The Impact of Globalization on North Carolina's Furniture Industries*. Raleigh: N.C. Department of Commerce, December 2002. https://cdm16062.contentdm.oclc.org/digital /collection/p249901coll22/id/642026

O'Hanlon, Thomas. "5,350 Companies = A Mixed-Up Furniture Industry." *Fortune*, February 1967, 145–59.

Oliver, J. L. *The Development and Structure of the Furniture Industry*. Oxford: Pergamon, 1966.

"Our Furniture Industry." *Winston-Salem Journal*, October 20, 1920.

"Outlook in Furniture Industry Very Bright." *Statesville (N.C.) Record and Landmark*, January 23, 1934.

Pogacar, Charlie. "White Family Tours the Lofts at White Furniture." *Mebane Enterprise*, December 10, 2015.

Patten, Eileen. "Racial, Gender Wage Gaps Persist in U.S. despite Some Progress." Pew Research Center, July 1, 2016. https://www.pewresearch.org/fact-tank /2016/07/01/racial-gender-wage-gaps-persist-in-u-s-despite-some-progress.

Patterson, James T. *Grand Expectations: The United States, 1945–1974*. New York: Oxford University Press, 1996.

Phillips, Laura A. W. "Thomasville Downtown Historic District, Thomasville, Davidson Co." National Register of Historic Places Nomination. Raleigh: N.C. State Historic Preservation Office, 2005. https://files.nc.gov/ncdcr/nr /DV0696.pdf.

"Picketing Grows More Popular at Local Factories." *High Point Enterprise*, August 22, 1919.

Pinchbeck, Raymond B. *The Virginia Negro Artisan and Tradesman*. Richmond, Va.: William Byrd, 1926.

"Plan B Scratched, City Misses Visit by Kennedy." *High Point Enterprise*, September 18, 1960.

"Plants Consolidate." *Wilmington Morning Star*, August 19, 1911.

Plice, Steven S. *Manpower and Merger: The Impact of Merger upon Personnel Policies in the Carpet and Furniture Industries*. Philadelphia: University of Pennsylvania Press, 1976.

Pocket Directory of the Furniture Manufacturers of the Southern States, Including Allied Lines. High Point, N.C.: Furniture Press, 1923.

"Professor of New Furniture Course at State Appointed." *Rocky Mount Telegram*, May 12, 1949.

"Protest a Project of Mrs. Roosevelt." *New York Times*, February 21, 1934.

Randolph Technical Institute. *Randolph Technical Institute General Catalog, 1977–79*. Asheboro, N.C.: Randolph Technical Institute, 1977.

Ransom, Frank Edward. *The City Built on Wood: A History of the Furniture Industry in Grand Rapids, Michigan, 1850–1950*. Ann Arbor, Mich.: Edwards Brothers, 1955.

Rauschenberg, Bradford L. "A Study of Baroque and Gothic-Style Gravestones in Davidson County, North Carolina." *Journal of Early Southern Decorative Arts* 3, no. 2 (1977): 24–50.

Ready, Milton. *The Tar Heel State: A New History of North Carolina*. Columbia: University of South Carolina Press, 2020.

"Respecting Distress of Local Company." *High Point Enterprise*, June 26, 1942.

The Role of the Small Businessman. Washington, D.C.: U.S. Government Printing Office, 1976.

Rowland, Ed. "Furniture Manufacturers Can't Keep Up with Orders." *Daily Times-News* (Burlington, N.C.), December 17, 1972.

Sasso, Michael. "Lost Factory Jobs of North Carolina Are Gone for Good, but Few Seem to Mind." *Bloomberg*, August 27, 2019.

Saunders, William, ed., *The Colonial Records of North Carolina*. 2 vols. Raleigh: P. M. Hale, 1886.

Savas, Lisa Plummer. "High Point Market Holds Safe Fall Show Despite Lower-Than-Usual Attendance." *Trade Show News Network* (Rosemont, IL), November 4, 2020. https://www.tsnn.com/news/high-point-market-holds -safe-fall-show-despite-lowerthanusual-attendance.

Schlichtman, John Joe. "Temp Town: The World's Most Prosperous Empty Downtown." PhD diss., New York University, 2005.

Schultz, Sue. "Polished-Up Market Finds Putting on Shine Is Costly." *Greensboro News and Record*, March 28, 2019.

Scott, Joan. Review of *Like a Family*, by Jacquelyn Dowd Hall, James L. Leloudis, Robert Rodgers Korstad, Mary Murphy, Lu Ann Jones, and Christopher B. Daly. *American Journal of Sociology* 94, no. 6 (1989): 1508–10.

"Scott to Visit Yugoslavia." *Winston-Salem Chronicle*, January 26, 1980.

Segal, Troy. "How to Identify Sheraton Style Antique Furniture." Spruce Crafts, August 18, 2019. https://www.thesprucecrafts.com/identifying-sheraton -style-furniture-148789.

Selby, John G. "'Better to Starve in the Shade than in the Factory': Labor Protest in High Point, North Carolina, in the Early 1930s." *North Carolina Historical Review* 61, no. 1 (1987): 43–64.

———. "Industrial Growth and Worker Protest in a New South City: High Point, North Carolina, 1859–1959." PhD diss., Duke University, 1984.

Seymour, Liz. "Cozy Is Not Comfy in High Point, N.C." *New York Times*, October 26, 1995. "Sheraton Name Wanted for Hotel." *High Point Enterprise*, September 2, 1920.

Silva, Kathryn M. "African American Millhands, the Durham Hosiery Mills, and the Politics of Race and Gender in Durham's Textile Industry, 1903–1920." *North Carolina Historical Review* 94, no. 1 (2017): 59–88.

"Sketch of J. Elwood Cox." *Times-Mercury* (Hickory, N.C.), September 3, 1908.

"Small Crowd Cheers LBJ during Whistle-Stop Here." *High Point Enterprise*, October 11, 1960.

Small, John H. "State of North Carolina—Forest and Mineral Resources." *Asheville Weekly Citizen*, July 4, 1902.

Smart, Ben. "Guests From 100+ Countries Descend on High Point for World -Famous Furniture Market." *WFMY* (Greensboro, N.C.), October 16, 2021.

Smialek, Jeanna. "North Carolina's Furniture Hub Is Booming. What Comes Next?" *New York Times*, November 27, 2021.

"Southern Furniture Manufacturing." *County Record* (Kingstree, S.C.), July 25, 1901.

"Southern States Increasing Lead in Several Fields of Furniture Making." *Furniture South*, April 1929, 30–31.

Steelman, Joseph F. "Republicanism in North Carolina: John Motley Morehead's Campaign to Revive a Moribund Party, 1908–1910." *North Carolina Historical Review* 42, no. 2 (1965), 153–68.

Stevens, William. *Anvil of Adversity: Biography of a Furniture Pioneer*. Kingsport, Tenn.: Kingsport, 1968.

Stoesen, Alexander R. *Guilford County: A Brief History*. Raleigh: Historical Publications Section, N.C. Division of Archives and History, 1993.

"Strike Situation Quieter in State." *Statesville (N.C.) Record and Landmark*, September 23, 1932.

Styers, Reginald. "Good Afternoon." *High Point Enterprise*, May 20, 1969.

"Tar Heel Liberals Have a Day of Victory." *Independent* (Elizabeth City, N.C.), September 30, 1932.

"TFI Is Closing Chicago Display." *High Point Enterprise*, March 21, 1971.

"T. H. Broyhill Walking Park." Visit Hickory Metro, 2021. https://www .visithickorymetro.com/listing/t-h-broyhill-walking-park/1306.

"Things to Do and Places to Go." *Daily Times-News* (Burlington, N.C.), October 8, 1977.

Thomas, David N. "Getting Started in High Point," *Forest History Newsletter* 11, no. 2 (1967): 23–32.

Thomas, David Nolan. "Early History of the North Carolina Furniture Industry, 1880–1921." PhD diss., University of North Carolina, Chapel Hill, 1964.

"Thomasville to Erect Big Chair on Commons." *Dispatch* (Lexington, N.C.), February 13, 1922.

"Thomasville Is Interested in Fate of C & Y R.R." *Twin-City Daily Sentinel* (Winston-Salem, N.C.), November 11, 1922.

"Tobacco Stemming Workers' Age Does Not Rule Output, United States House Hears." *Daily Times-News* (Burlington, N.C.), March 21, 1940.

"To Make Iron Beds." *Weekly High Point Enterprise*, January 8, 1902.

Tomlinson of High Point. *Furniture by Tomlinson*. Catalog. [High Point, N.C.], 1942. https://archive.org/details/furniturebytomli00toml/mode/2up.

"Tomlinson of High Point." *The State* (Raleigh, N.C.), January 6, 1945.

Toner, Robin. "Incumbency: Asset or No?" *New York Times*, August 15, 1986.

Trincia, Andy. "Furniture Sales Slump This Year." *Daily Tar Heel* (Chapel Hill, N.C.), December 5, 1984.

Tryon Palace. "Furniture Collection," June 2021. https://www.tryonpalace.org
/wp-content/uploads/2021/06/furniture.pdf.

"Undergraduate Catalog 1977–1979." *North Carolina State University Bulletin* (December 1976).

"Union Is Rejected in Drexel Election." *News Herald* (Morganton, N.C.), January 16, 1970.

"Unionists Pickett Few Local Plants, Results Not Known." *High Point Enterprise*, August 20, 1919.

"Union Loses 1st Election in Caldwell." *Charlotte Observer* (Charlotte, N.C.), March 10, 1978.

"The United Furniture Company." *Dispatch* (Lexington, N.C.), May 5, 1921.

University of North Carolina, Greensboro. *One-Hundred-and-Twenty-Eighth Annual University Catalog, 2019–2020.* https://catalog.uncg.edu/Archive /2019-2020.pdf.

U.S. Census Bureau. *Fifteenth Census of the United States: Manufactures, Reports by States, Statistics for Industrial Areas, Counties, and Cities.* Washington, D.C.: Government Printing Office, 1933.

———. *Fifteenth Census of the United States: Population, General Report on Occupations.* Washington, D.C.: Government Printing Office, 1933.

———. *Fifteenth Census of the United States: Population, Number and Distribution of Inhabitants.* Washington, D.C.: Government Printing Office, 1931.

———. *Fifteenth Census of the United States: Population, Occupations, by States, Reports by States, Giving Statistics for Cities of 25,000 or More.* Washington, D.C.: Government Printing Office, 1933.

———. *Fourteenth Census of the United States: North Carolina, Statistics of Population, Occupations, Agriculture, Drainage, Manufactures, and Mines and Quarries for the State, Counties, and Cities.* Washington, D.C.: Government Printing Office, 1925.

———. *Thirteenth Census of the United States: Statistics for North Carolina, Containing Statistics of Population, Agriculture, Manufactures, and Mining for the State, Counties, Cities, and Other Divisions.* Washington, D.C.: Department of Commerce, 1914.

———. *Twelfth Census of the United States: Manufactures, States and Territories.* Washington, D.C.: Government Printing Office, 1902.

U.S. Economic Analysis Bureau. "Full-Time and Part-Time Employees: Domestic Private Industries: Manufacturing: Durable Goods: Furniture and Fixtures." https://fred.stlouisfed.org/series/J4216C0A173NBEA.

U.S. Federal Bureau of Investigation. "FBI Releases 2019 Crime Statistics." News release, September 28, 2020. https://www.fbi.gov/news/pressrel /press-releases/fbi-releases-2019-crime-statistics.

"U.S. Furniture Industries." *Tribunal Aid* (High Point, N.C.), August 29, 1973.

U.S. Justice Department. "Crime in the United States by Volume and Rate per 100,000 Inhabitants, 1991–2010." Uniform Crime Reporting, Federal Bureau of Investigation, September 2011. https://ucr.fbi.gov/crime-in-the-u.s/2010 /crime-in-the-u.s.-2010/tables/10tbl01.xls.

U.S. Labor Department. *Employment, Hours, and Earnings, States and Areas, 1939–82.* Vol. 2, *New Hampshire–Wyoming.* Washington, D.C.: Government Printing Office, 1984. https://fraser.stlouisfed.org/title/245/item/497801/content/pdf /bls_1370-17_v2_1984.

———. *Wages and Hours of Labor in Cotton-Goods Manufacturing, 1910 to 1930.* Washington, D.C.: Government Printing Office, June 1931. https://fraser .stlouisfed.org/title/3913/item/493152.

———. *Wages and Hours of Labor in the Furniture Industry, 1910 to 1929.* Washington, D.C.: Government Printing Office, January 1931. https://fraser.stlouisfed .org/title/3921/item/493170.

U.S. Labor Statistics Bureau. "All Employees, Manufacturing." https://fred .stlouisfed.org/series/MANEMP.

———. "State and Area Employment, Hours, and Earnings: North Carolina, Manufacturing Employment, All Employees, in Thousands," 2012–22. https://data .bls.gov/timeseries/SMS37000003000000001?amp%253bdata_tool =XGtable&output_view=data&include_graphs=true.

U.S. National Labor Relations Board. *Decisions and Orders of the National Labor Relations Board.* Vol. 55, *February 24–April 24, 1944.* Washington, D.C.: Government Printing Office, 1944.

———. *Decisions and Orders of the National Labor Relations Board.* Vol. 37, *November 20–December 31, 1941.* Washington, D.C.: Government Printing Office, 1942.

Vanderburg, Timothy W. *Cannon Mills and Kannapolis: Persistent Paternalism in a Textile Town.* Knoxville: University of Tennessee Press, 2013.

Van Deusen, John George. *The Black Man in White America.* Washington, D.C.: Associated Publishers, 1944.

Vogel, Carol. "Home Design; High Point's New Verve." April 29, 1984.

"Volume $25,000,000 at Furniture Show." *New York Times*, July 31, 1938.

"Vote for Union." *Statesville (N.C.) Record and Landmark*, August 26, 1964.

Waggoner, Martha. "N.C. Revises Its Civil War Death Rolls Downward." *Free Lance-Star* (Fredericksburg, Va.), September 19, 2019.

Wainwright, Oliver. "Shiny, Happy Households: Formica Turns 100." *Guardian*, January 17, 2013.

"A Waiting Game on at High Point." *North Carolinian* (Raleigh, N.C.), April 5, 1906.

Wear, Anne Flynn. "Coley Home Acquires N.C. Manufacturing Facility." *Furniture*

Today, November 12, 2021. https://www.furnituretoday.com/e-commerce
/coley-home-acquires-n-c-manufacturing-facility.

Weems, Robert E., and Lewis A. Randolph. "The National Response to Richard M.
Nixon's Black Capitalism Initiative: The Success of Domestic Détente." *Journal
of Black Studies* 32, no. 1 (2001): 66–83.

Western Carolina University. *Current 2021–2022 Undergraduate Catalog*. http://
catalog.wcu.edu/index.php?catoid=52.

"When J. Elwood Cox Showed His Unfitness." *North Carolinian* (Raleigh, N.C.),
September 17, 1908.

Whitcomb, Dorothy. "Hickory Springs Eyes Innovation, Diversification."
BedTimes, March 1, 2009. https://bedtimesmagazine.com/2009/03
/hickory-springs-eyes-innovation-diversification.

*White Directory of Manufacturers of Furniture and Kindred Goods of the United
States, British Provinces, and Mexico*. Grand Rapids, Mich.: White Printing,
1901. https://archive.org/details/whitedirectoryofoogran.

White Furniture Company. *From Generation to Generation*. Mebane, N.C.: White
Furniture, 1981.

White Furniture Company. *34 Years at It: The White Furniture Company*. Mebane,
N.C.: White Furniture, 1914.

"White's Furniture." *Daily Times-News* (Burlington, N.C.), February 6, 1961.

Whittington, Jerry L., and Ronald A. Hoover. *High Point, North Carolina, 1900–
1910: A Bicentennial Souvenir*. High Point, N.C.: n.p., 1910.

Wood, Elizabeth. "Modern Furniture Here to Stay." *Furniture South*, September
1929, 11.

"Wood Furniture Concentration Growing." *High Point Enterprise*, August 15, 1974.

"Wood Salutes: J. E. Broyhill." *Wood and Wood Products*, August 1957.

Woodward, C. Vann. *Origins of the New South, 1877–1913*. Baton Rouge: Louisiana
State University Press, 1951.

"WPA Furniture Making Fought." *Hickory Daily Record*, August 27, 1936.

"Wrecked Plane and Dead Pilot Finally Found." *Robesonian* (Lumberton, N.C.),
November 10, 1961.

Wright, Gavin. Review of *Like a Family*, by Jacquelyn Dowd Hall, James L. Leloudis, Robert Rodgers Korstad, Mary Murphy, Lu Ann Jones, and Christopher B.
Daly. *Journal of Interdisciplinary History* 19, no. 4 (1989): 697–99.

Wrong, Elaine Gale. *The Negro in the Apparel Industry*. Philadelphia: Industrial Research Unit, Wharton School, University of Pennsylvania, 1974.

"Yancey County Manufacturing Plant to Close." *WLOS* (Asheville, N.C.), February
17, 2020.

"Year 'round Exhibitors at the Southern Market." *Furniture South*, January 1931, 37.

Yokely, C. E. "Current Cycle." *Carolinian* (Raleigh, N.C.), July 30, 1949.

INDEX

Printed in the USA
CPSIA information can be obtained
at www.ICGtesting.com
LVHW041733241023
761957LV00004BA/413